COMPETING ON VALUE

COMPETING
ON
VALUE

Mack Hanan and Peter Karp

amacom
American Management Association

Library of Congress Cataloging-in-Publication Data
Hanan, Mack.
     Competing on value /
  Mack Hanan and Peter Karp.
       p.   cm.
  Includes index.
  ISBN 0-8144-5036-9
  1. Marketing management. 2. Pricing. I. Karp, Peter.
  II. Title.
  HF5415.13.H28   1991
  658.8'16—dc20   90-22951
                                              CIP

Printing number

10   9   8   7   6   5   4   3   2   1

To Don Massaro, who asked us the right question:
"What do I need you for?"
We told him:
"So that your own people will have the right answer when your customers ask them the same question."

Contents

Preface

How many times has this happened to you?

You are sitting across from a major customer. He tells you that he is considering awarding 100 percent of your category's purchases to you or to your number one competitor. He agrees that your product has a quality advantage and he may prefer certain other aspects about dealing with your company. But your competitor has made a significantly lower price offer and, after all, the quality difference between the two of you is not all that great. Your product may be superior but your competitor's product is good enough. If you can see your way clear to meeting his price, which is discounted by 25 percent compared to your own discount of 15 percent, the customer might be predisposed to favor you. Otherwise, you will probably be out of the picture for the next twelve to thirty-six months.

What do you do? Hold your margins, which are already discounted, and risk losing the business—and perhaps losing the customer as well—or do you buy volume business at a low-profit or no-profit price? In situations like this, you must have thought time and again how advantageous it would be if you could avoid this kind of no-win scenario or figure out a third alternative to losing business or losing profits. There is a third alternative, but it requires a very different selling strategy.

Using Exhibits A and B of Value

Instead of sitting across from a major customer, you are sitting side by side, the way partners do. The customer is different, too. Instead of being a purchaser, he or she is a manager of either a customer business function or a line of business that you can affect—in other words, a cost-center manager or a profit-center manager. You have only two things to show and tell, neither of which will be your product or service. One of your demonstrations, Exhibit A, is a 3×5 card that contains either the average range within which you normally can reduce the key cost contributions made by the manager's business function or, if the manager runs a line of business, the average range within which you normally can increase such a business's contributions to sales and earnings. These are your *norms*. Each of them represents the values you typically contribute to similar customers.

The card compares your values in each category of cost or revenue contribution with the customer's industry average and, to the extent that you can know it, the customer's own current standard of performance. Compare our norms against your own, you say. Compare them against those of your competitors who make up the industry average. Tell me, what would it be worth to you if we can work together to bring you closer to our norms—how many dollars of saved costs or realized revenues and earnings would be generated by each one percent of improvement? What would it be worth to you to get them?

By daring the customer to take your "norm challenge," you force him to reveal where he needs improvements in his competitive advantage. Either he will want to be a lower-cost producer or a higher-market shareholder or profit maker. By asking him to quantify the added value of becoming more competitively advantaged, you induce him to create an objective for you to work toward together. And by asking him to calculate its worth, you invite him to put a price on what he will pay to achieve his objective. Then you show him Exhibit B.

This exhibit is a model proposal of how you normally improve the contribution of a comparable customer's business function or line of business to customer profits. The proposal is an actual proposal that you have rendered anonymous or a composite based on an amalgam of your experience or, if you have never prepared such a proposal before, a conservative projection of what you believe your capability to be.

The proposal presents a customer's realization from a business function or line of business on a before-and-after basis. First you present its current contribution to costs or revenues before you begin to work together. Then you show the contribution from the improved cash flows that result from your work. You show the customer's lower costs or his higher margins or volume, how long it took to achieve the improved results, and what the net impacts have been on customer profits, cash flow, and productivity.

What-Iffing Your Way to Value

What if, you ask the customer, we can work together to achieve a similar result for you? If you are interested in learning how much improvement we can make to the profit contribution of your own operation, we will prepare a customized proposal, using your own numbers, specifically for you. Once you accept it and we get it funded, we can start immediately to make you more competitively advantaged.

This strategy for selling is based on three prerequisites: You must know your value. You must price your value. And you must sell your value. Unless you know your value, you cannot sell it. If you do not know your value, all you can sell is your cost. If you cannot price your value, all you can price is your cost. Your customers and your competitors will drive you back to your cost every chance you give them. As a result, two catastrophic events will take place:

1. Your own sales process will competitively disadvantage you by either costing you sales or your proper margins on them.
2. Your customers will have less of an advantage over their own competitors because the only improvements you will make to their operations will come from selling to them at giveaway prices, thereby re-

ducing their costs of acquisition. Their costs of ownership, that is, the life cycle costs that can exceed
acquisition costs several hundredfold, will never benefit from your applications, information, education,
implementation, or consultation expertise. Or, if they
do, they will typically do so at no value to you because
you will give your benefits away in order to sweeten
your giveaway price even further.

In the 1990s, if you sell products on their price-performance specifications, anyone who competes against you
on the basis of value will have the advantage.

If you sell product features and benefits—what goes into
your products rather than the values that come out of
them—you will suffer a similar disadvantage, just as you will
if your business objectives are to grow your own sales and
market share instead of the sales and market shares of your
major customers, reduce your own costs instead of reducing
customer costs, and surpass your own competitors instead of
helping your customers achieve their own competitive advantage.

If you push product, you will be mercilessly pushed on
margin. Without margin control, how will you grow? If you
say with volume, how will you fund its costs? If you say with
cash flow, your margins will have to come from cost control.
What kind of business will you be: sales up, profits down?
How will you grow? How will you grow your people? How
will you grow your customers and suppliers? If you do not
grow them, who will grow you?

Making Value Unaffordable to Be Without

Customers who buy from you but leave you profitless are
telling you that your price exceeds their perception of your
value. They are sending you a message to equalize them. But
if you do not know your value, you cannot price it. If your
customers do not know your value either, they cannot per-

ceive it. They will end up taking it from you. You will end up giving it away.

On the other hand, a customer who knows your value will have no trouble affording it because he knows that it represents a good investment. He will always get more back than he pays out. As a matter of fact, he will not think in terms of affording your value. He will not be able to afford doing without it.

The best customers you can have—the customers you must have if you are going to ensure the growth of your business—are customers who *cannot afford to do without your value*. This means that they must know it and respect the contribution that it makes to their competitive advantage. They must know you as its source.

They must come to depend on your value, to factor it into their plans, and commit to it as a part of their planned business objectives. Once you have proved your dependability as a value-adder, your customers will rely on your value. Once they rely on it, they will not be able to afford to do without it.

When that occurs, your competitors' proposed values will appear to be unaffordable no matter how cheap their price may be because they will seem to be less reliable—that is, their reliability will be less proved and therefore cannot be depended on to replace you. Two kinds of potential losses will stare your customer in the face. One is the opportunity loss of your future values. The other is the immediate loss of his competitive objectives.

Avoiding the Penalty for Not Knowing

Many suppliers excuse themselves from selling value by saying that they have no choice. They accept what they call "the theoretical argument" based on value, but they continue to sell on the basis of cost. Cost is easy for them to know because it is internal, whereas their value is unknown to them because it takes place outside their awareness or control in the belly of the operations of their customers. These sup-

pliers are saying that their sales process stops with the customer's signature on an order, that their customers' businesses are terra incognita to them, and that they would have
to know "more about a customer's business than even the
customer knows" in order to propose and deliver measurable
added values to it.

Managers who think this way are prime candidates for
the "ignorance tax" imposed on their margins for not knowing the value they represent.

It is a fact of business life that all suppliers deliver value.
If they did not, they would not be in business. Tomorrow's
competition, however, will belong not to unknowing deliver-
ers of value but to suppliers who know how much value they
can deliver, who price their value, and who sell it. If you are
an unknowing deliverer of value, one of two things will be
true: You and your customers will both be ignorant of your
value and you will therefore never be able to claim the full
margins that it can justify. You will never be safe from
competitors, who do not have to be better than you in any
significant way but simply sell at a lower price.

The second possibility is that your customers will know
your value but you will not. Even though your value would
justify full margins or make price-reducing deals and free
services unnecessary, your customers will not tell you. They
will go on doing business with you as if you are a cost to be
reduced rather than a value to be fairly rewarded. You will
lose two ways, rendering free value yet still sacrificing your
margins.

You can sell on value no matter what business you are
in. You have only two questions to answer:

1. What critical success factors do we affect in our
   customers' business functions or lines of business that
   are crucial to their competitive advantage?
2. How do we affect them most significantly: by displac-
   ing or constraining some of their costs or enhancing
   their revenues, earnings, or market shares?

The answers you come up with will determine the three
most important decisions you can make about your business:

1. What you want to be compared against: your competitors' prices or your customers' current values
2. Where you want to attach your price: to your products or to the added values you represent to your customers
3. Who you want to make your buying decisions: customer purchasing managers who buy on price or business managers who live or die on value

If you still run a traditional business, or if you run an innovative business traditionally, you probably do not know your value. When you sell, you know your products and services, their features and benefits, and their terms and conditions. As a customer, you know how much you pay. But what about the value of what you buy and sell: What about its contributions to your own growth and to the growth of your customers? What about how much you are adding to your competitive advantage and to theirs? Your managers will probably assure you that they know the values they add. You will be tempted to reassure yourself by speculating that, surely, your customers know your value. There is one quick way to find out.

Ask your managers if they will risk being paid a percentage of the values they add to your customers, and nothing more. Then you will know their value and what they know of it. So will they.

COMPETING
ON
VALUE

1

The Value Strategy

In the American economy during most of the twentieth century, with its industrial manufacturing base and preoccupation with learning curves of low-cost production and mass commodity product marketing, margins were the innovator's privilege. Once market share became an overarching objective, margins had to be traded away as the price of industry leadership. Under competitive pressure to gain share and hold it, many managers came to believe that they had to choose from two basic business strategies:

1. Hold margins but give up market share and lose both volume and profits.
2. Give margins away to meet price competition, lose profits, but hold onto market share and its volume that keeps costs down.

Either way, unit margins became the price of growth. Maturity, if you could get to it, would pay you back in cash flow but it would be marginless.

Volume, of course, also had its costs: costs of materials and energy, costs of manufacturing and labor, and costs of sales, all of which ate into cash flow and turned even the most trivial price changes into critical success factors for many businesses. As the economy has shifted its base away from industry to services and as business downsizing, prod-

uct-line rationalizing, and industrial restructuring have occurred parallel with increasingly finite market segmentation
on the demand side, mass has been disappearing from both
sides of the equation. Unit profits have become popular again
and comments are frequently heard that "our job is to
squeeze every bit of margin out of every business we have"
and "today's task is to maximize profits on lower levels of
volume."

IBM has summed up its vision of the new realities of
business this way: "As parts of the computer industry become
increasingly commodity-like—where price becomes the main
factor—you will see the IBM Company departing from those
parts. *We are in the business of high-margin sales.*"

The business of high-margin sales is the business of high
value-based sales. Only high value added to your customers'
businesses can command high margins. The best way—in
many industries, the only way—to make money is to put a
new emphasis on value. How can your new businesses make
sure that they can claim their full margins and not leave any
appreciable percentage of them on the table? How can your
mature businesses hold onto margins even under parity
product competition or, if margins have already been sacri-
ficed to volume, how can they be regained?

In other words, how can the value that must be the base
of your margins be known, priced, and sold?

*Value is the added competitive advantage you bring to your
customers.* Whenever you contribute to reducing a customer's
costs, you add to his competitive advantage as a lower-cost
supplier. Similarly, you become a contributor to his competitive market leadership whenever you help expand his revenues and earnings.

When a customer subtracts the costs he incurs to do
business with you from the results they add to his competitiveness, the sum that is left over is your value. When your
added values are *significant, safe,* and *successive,* you become a
supplier of your customer's growth.

From your customers' perspective, adding to their value
is your sole reason for being in business. It is what your

customers mean, even if you do not, by customer satisfaction. Customers are not satisfied by your quality, but only by the value they can get out of it. Nor are customers satisfied by your technological superiority, your support services, or your products; they are satisfied only by the added value they can confer on their competitive advantage. How much does your quality add to a customer's ability to be a low-cost producer? How much do your support services add to a customer's ability to be a higher-volume or high-margin supplier? These are the true measures of customer satisfaction because they measure the values on which satisfaction is based.

Selling is transacting value. It is the way you add to your own value by first adding value to your customers—not adding products, which represent only the transfer of your costs, but adding the positive values of your products' contributions to customer profits. Each sale should enable you and your customers to end up with new values. Do you know how much new value each sale realizes for you and for your customer? Do you know how soon it is realized? Do you know what the rates of return are on the customer's investment to acquire it and on your investment to sell it?

If you do not know your value, you cannot price it. If you cannot price it, you cannot sell it. If you cannot sell it, you will be reduced to selling the products and services that contribute to it. Your price will reflect their costs instead of their values. Because cost-based prices are always lower than value-based prices, you will earn less on each value exchange. Your own competitive advantage will suffer. So will your growth. If you cost-base your prices against a competitor who knows his value and prices his value and sells his value, you will have a name for him. You will call him the industry leader.

If, at some future date, you discover that your own value actually exceeds your competitor's value but neither you nor your customers have known about it, you will have a name for yourself, too.

Value-Basing Your Competitiveness

The competition of the 1990s is nonproduct competition. Products no longer compete because, for the most part, they have reached an "equality of quality" at similarly high levels of performance. They all meet open standards. As a result, there will be hardly any way to distinguish between them. Customer fiat, based on the need to achieve maximum cost-effectiveness through universal interconnection, interaction, and integration, enforces a universal commoditization of product performance. Homogeneous specifications enforce homogeneous capabilities. Product margins accordingly shrink to the level of commodity margins. Competition erodes them further, rather than enhancing them.

This is true as a direct result of qualitative excellence across the board. Standards of performance among many competitors will reach or approach the paramount rating of six sigma, virtual perfection with a defect rate of only 3.4 parts per million. As a result, quality will virtually disappear as a competitive advantage. It will no longer differentiate suppliers in any meaningful way. Why will a quality standard of 99.9997 be more competitively advantageous to a customer, and therefore to his supply partner, than 99.9996? Why will a customer pay more for it—and if he does, how much more?

In many cases, quality at these near-perfect levels will exceed most customer requirements for "good enoughness." Unless a customer's "point of sufficient return" is known, where his satisfaction is optimized, the supermaximization of quality over and above that point will simply represent unnecessary and often unrecoverable cost. It may yield temporary bragging rights. But it may also contribute negatively to a supplier's own competitive advantage by making him a higher-cost supplier while contributing no advantageous value to his customers.

Because equality has come to quality, defect-free products have become the rule and not an exception. They are one of the basic requirements of competition rather than a competitive advantage. The absence of competitive product quality will keep a supplier from even getting in the door. But, once he is in, quality acts merely as his entry fee. All it does is allow him to line up for the race. At that moment, competition begins. The winner is the supplier who delivers not the highest-quality product, but the highest quantity of customer value. These are not necessarily one and the same.

Quality is what goes into your products. Value is what your customers get out of them. Manufacturing-based and process-driven companies cherish the belief that they build in value. In actuality, they build in costs. At best, these costs only enable customers to extract value, to get out what is inside. This requires more than zero defects. It requires a dedication to help customers maximize their ability to derive value by training and education, information, application, and consultation. These are the capabilities that comprise value.

A company that achieves six sigma in manufacturing will suffer competitive disadvantage unless it can also achieve six sigma in its value-extracting capabilities. On the other hand, a company with six sigma standards of performance as an applier and counselor will be competitively advantaged over any other company that lacks them no matter how qualified its product may be.

What does product quality contribute to value? The answer to this question will determine how much quality must be built into a product. How can product quality best be extracted and put to work for your customers? The answer to this question will determine the quality that must be built into your information and application capabilities.

Customer satisfaction is a measure of applied values, not engineered or manufactured values. Satisfaction takes place in the customer's premises, not his supplier's. It reflects the customer's competitive advantage, not an advantage proclaimed by a supplier who has added another integer to the right of the decimal point in measuring his quality. Satisfaction measures the customer's added value—how much more competitive he is, how much less of a high-cost producer or how much more of a cost-effective, high-share marketer.

Satisfaction cannot be engineered in. It can only be coun-
seled out, trained out, and applied out.

Putting Customers Before Shareholders

One of the most enduring platitudes in business is the
dedication renewed by each generation of managers to create
the most value for their shareholders. Other than that, very
little is generally said about value. Most managers talk about
their products or processes: how they make what they sell
and how they sell what they make. Even managers who are
proud of being customer-driven talk of shipping products
and stocking and shelving products rather than shipping
and installing value.

In reality, shareholder value is derived value. It is derived from value that must first be delivered to customers,
because they are the source of all value in business. Only in
return for the values you add to your customers can your
shareholders receive value from your business. Customer
value comes first. Shareholder value is a second derivative.

If you position your business to add customer values,
shareholder values will follow. The converse, however, is not
automatically true.

A business committed to value improvement for customers operates with a unique mindset. Its managers ask the
question "What is the customer value?" about every investment they contemplate. They preoccupy themselves with all
the issues that are related to value:

- Does this investment opportunity give us the biggest
  value bang for the buck or are there better options?
- Would a smaller investment yield a "good enough"
  value? What is the incremental contribution of each
  added dollar of investment beyond the "good enough"
  point? Where is the point of no appreciably enhanced
  return?
- Will this added value give our customers an increased
  competitive advantage in cost management? In reve-

nue management? How much of an advantage? How soon will it accrue? When will it come on stream—when will it reach payback? What will it return on its investment for our customers and for us?

A value-based mindset like this can serve as a screen of criteria for allocating your resources to products, processes, services, organization structures, and operating practices and policies. They can help guide your investment schedule, signaling priorities where the customer values are greatest. They can bring your customers into your management process, putting their values foremost in your plans and, just as important, letting them know it. This will cause you to attend to one more issue at the time you make each major decision:

- Where does this added value rank in our customers' satisfaction with us? Is it on their "must list"?
- If so, will it help us maximize our margins?
- If not, why should we go ahead with it?

Classifying the Specifications of Value

Customers are preoccuied with value. When they are presented with value that they can add to their business, they interpret it as an investment signal. Before they bet their money, they need to know how much value they will gain in relation to how much they will be required to invest. Their answer will be a composite of two functions: the dollar value and the time value of the investment's return.

How much value will be the outcome of each investment? This is every customer's qualifying question that each sales proposal must clear. The height of the bar is set at the customer's hurdle rate, the minimal rate of return he can accept for his investments, which is determined by his cost of capital. If the return he gets back on an investment of capital is less than his cost to amass the capital in the first place, and therefore less than its value, he cannot make the investment.

A customer's acceptable suppliers are those who clear his hurdle rate. His partnered suppliers clear it consistently with the greatest margins. That is their initial criterion for partnership.

How much value will be returned is one of the three specifications that customers apply to judging the compelling nature of an investment. It enables them to make a yes or no judgment about whether an investment should be made at all. It also permits a comparative judgment about which of several potential investments should be made first, second, and third or pigeonholed indefinitely.

All customers want to maximize their returns. The more each dollar earns, the better. But the quicker it earns more, even better. The *time value of money* is money's second specification. Customers know that time is money. A dollar today is always worth more to them than the same dollar tomorrow. It can be said, conversely, that money is time. A proposed return of $1.50 for every $1.00 invested to earn it is meaningless without specifying how soon the return will accrue. If it takes 100 days, the deal may be interesting. But 100 years is no deal at all.

There are two dimensions to the soonness of a customer's return. One is the time to payback of the investment. This determines when the customer is no longer at risk for the principal amount of his investment. At payback, he is clean. He has his original funds back and he can reinvest them to make more money. But customers do not invest just to pay themselves back. The fact that money has a time value ensures that a loss will be incurred if payback is all that a customer gets in return for an investment. The loss comes from forsaking the opportunity to have made more money if the same amount of funds has been invested somewhere else—in a different proposal or with a different proposer. The second dimension of soonness is how quickly the full net value of the customer's investment is realized. This represents his total incremental value.

Muchness and soonness are mythical without sureness, which is why certainty of the dollar and time values you sell is the third specification of value. Without certainty that you will add the amount of value you propose to his business within the time you propose to add it, your customer will not be able to rely on it. Without reliance, he will be unable to plan on reinvesting it for the next round of value-adding. He will be unable to take the next cycle of opportunities on the rise, when they are least costly and most opportune. He will not know for sure the total value of the assets he will have available and, as a consequence, how he will be able to allocate them. He will not know what new products or processes he can afford to invent, what he must acquire, or what he will have to divest.

Your certainty of how much value you can propose, and produce, and how soon you can produce it is summarized in your *norms*. They represent your averaged experience in adding value on an industry-specific, customer-function-specific, and solution-specific basis. When you flash your norms at a customer, you prove to him why you can be sure of your value. You have a track record. You have been where he is before. You know how he can improve and by how much.

Your norms speak for your standards of performance. If they are superior to your competition's norms, you can claim to be your industry standard. If they are superior to a customer's norms, you can claim to be his partner of choice.

After your norms say *why* you can be sure of your value, you must propose to your customers *how much* added value each of them can be sure of and *how soon* they can be sure they will receive it. Finally, you must do one more thing: You must prove *how sure* they can be.

Value can be differentiated in any of its three specifications. Your value can be greater than a competitor's. It can flow sooner, yielding positive cash by achieving payback earlier. Or it can be more certain. Muchness and soonness are a tradeoff. A customer's needs for them come and go on a problem-by-problem, opportunity-by-opportunity basis. Over time, all the value-adding proposals that a customer will receive from you and your competitors may well average out. But a customer's needs for sureness go on forever.

Your only continuing opportunity to differentiate your value is to stake out the claim to certainty. Even though customers always seek to maximize their returns, they learn quickly enough that a one percent difference in muchness or soonness between competitive proposals may not add up to as much as a one percent difference in their certainty. The best way for them to maximize their return over time is to be sure of your value.

Gaining and Losing Opportunities to Add Value

Your business, like every business, is both a customer and a supplier. In value terms, this means that you act as a buyer of other suppliers' values and a supplier of values to other buyers.

Each role is vital to your prosperity. If you are a poor shopper for values, you will end up being competitively disadvantaged in your own industry. To the extent that you offer noncompetitive values as a supplier, you will be further disadvantaged in your markets.

Figure 1-1 summarizes the competitive disparities between two similarly sized businesses in their roles as buyers of values. Each business is a customer of the same information technology supplier. Both businesses are making the same annual investment of $10 million, which represents an

Figure 1-1. Comparative value-to-price relationships.

	Business ABLE	Business BAKER
Annual Investment (price)	$10M	$10M
Incremental Profits (value)	$30M	$15M
Value per Dollar	$3	$1.5
Earnings-to-Investment Ratio	$3:1	$1.5:1

industry average of 2 percent of their gross sales, to automate their marketing functions. But there the similarities end.

Business ABLE is earning a 3-to-1 rate of return on its investment. The present value of the incremental profits directly attributable to its information technology systems is $30 million. On the other hand, business BAKER is earning only a 1.5-to-1 rate of return on the same investment. The present value of the incremental profits directly attributable to its information technology is half of competitor ABLE's.

Both businesses are receiving a positive return on their equal investments in automating their marketing information processes. Business ABLE is more competitive as a result. Business BAKER does not know that it is at a competitive disadvantage because it knows neither its own value nor the standard value for its industry. It is therefore a prime prospect for further value maximizing. So is business ABLE, but for a different reason: It cannot afford to have its value leadership equalized by a competitor.

Why is business BAKER unaware of the value it is receiving from marketing information technology? One reason is that BAKER's managers have never measured it. A second reason is that their supplier has never measured his contributions of value to the marketing functions of businesses like BAKER. Therefore he does not know his own norms or that his contribution to BAKER falls below them. If BAKER's managers find this out before he does, they may change suppliers because he has given them only half his potential value even though they have paid for all of it. This has left them with a significant opportunity loss.

Business BAKER's supplier is also incurring a significant opportunity loss. As Figure 1-1 shows, he has given away $2.5 million in value to business ABLE without pricing it any higher than his price to business BAKER. Yet ABLE is clearly receiving greater value. Unaware of his value as ABLE's supplier, he has sold the performance features and benefits of his information system on the basis of their price, not their value. At the same time, he is also losing the opportu-

nity to upgrade his sales to business ABLE on the basis of
their proven value.

Not knowing value, and therefore not being able to price it
or sell it, has led to four negative results in this typical
scenario:

1. Business ABLE will probably not increase its invest-
    ment with its supplier because it does not know how
    valuable each added dollar of investment can be.
2. Business BAKER will probably not increase its invest-
    ment with the supplier because it does not know it is
    competitively disadvantaged.
3. The supplier is at risk of losing business BAKER as a
    customer.
4. The supplier is leaving money on the table with
    business ABLE on the basis of his provable value.

Understanding How You Add Value

Of all the things you must know about your business, it is
most essential to know how you add value to your customers.
What kind of value-adder are you, the kind who helps his
customers reduce or avoid variable costs so that their prices
can be lowered and their margins thereby improved? Or do
you help customers improve margins by adding new features
and benefits to their products, services, or systems? Or do
you help expand market share by adding to productivity?
    In order to be a value-adder, you must know how to
help your customers control one or more of their critical
costs or exploit one or more of their critical revenue sources.
What is your value arena? Is it your customers' R&D, engineering, manufacturing, or marketing functions? If it is
R&D, do you add value to materials testing or to the product
design cycle? If it is manufacturing, do you add value to
production scheduling or quality control? If it is marketing,
do you add value to order entry or inventory? What type of
leverage do you exert? Do you help customers speed up their

operations or perform them better or more cheaply? How much faster or better or more cheaply?

What are you expert in? When you penetrate a customer's business, where can you make a predicable positive impact on his competitiveness? How worthwhile will it be to both of you?

The worthwhileness of your values will be easy for customers to calculate. It can be the dollar value that accrues to one of their new products when it is able to enter its market ninety days sooner than its business plan proposes or if it can reach breakeven six months sooner. Or it can be the dollar value that accrues to an established business when it is able to maintain its margins one year longer at maturity.

No matter what critical success business or critical success function of a customer business you can affect, the major qualifying question will be: Do you affect the most critical factors in each function? This is where the money is. With a new product, do you make sure the product is being driven by its most likely market? With a growth business, can you help fulfill the complete market opportunity offered to the business and avoid the opportunity loss from missing out on additional attainable profits? In maturity, can you maintain margins longer for a customer's business or help it to regenerate its growth to regain competitiveness? It will not be enough to say, "Yes, we do these things." This qualifies you only as an alternate vendor. You must be able to say, "We do these things *best*." Only in this way can you become the industry standard for your values.

Competitive advantages come to your customers from lower costs and increased earnings capability. Costs break out into two major categories: materials, including their handling, shipping, and storage, which can account for up to 20 percent of total costs and are the primary candidates for savings; and labor, which is no longer the main variable cost because it averages only 8 to 12 percent of total production costs.

In contrast to cost reduction, revenues and earnings can be increased in several ways. Getting a current product to market faster by accelerating its order processing cycle can

Figure 1-2. Common competitive advantages and disadvantages.

Common Competitive Advantages	Common Competitive Disadvantages
• Foreshortened turnaround time starting with order entry and proceeding through manufacturing and delivery • Just-in-time inventory • Reduced rework and recall due to close approximation of zero defects • Foreshortened new product development cycle	• Excessive inventories and high costs associated with their management • Late shipments and resulting lengthened collection cycle • Impeded materials flow and consequent loss of productivity • Foreshortened product life cycles that cause early maturing of margins and create need to recover investments faster

step up its sales. Getting new products developed and marketed faster can do the same. Improving products and services and their value-to-price ratios can result in greater sales through enhanced satisfaction of your customers' customers.

No matter whether you are lowering a customer's costs or increasing his earnings capability, you should ask two questions of every opportunity to add value:

1. Where are cost savings and productivity improvements possible?
2. Where are volume and margin increases possible?

These questions should be asked first about all the common advantages and disadvantages that affect customer competitiveness that you deal with every day. A checklist of them appears in Figure 1-2. Then you can move on to more sophisticated areas of adding value, such as these:

- Where are cost savings and earnings increases possible on a product-specific basis? On a product-specific/market-specific basis?
- Where are cost savings and earnings increases possible in the total life cycle costs on a product-specific basis? On a product-specific/market-specific basis?
- Where are cost savings and earnings increases possible on an operation-specific basis? On an operation-specific/product-specific basis?

Asking Value-Based Questions

The beginning of wisdom in competing on value is to know your markets' needs for values and to make certain that you become a major contributor to them. This is different from being a major source of product supply. It is also different from being a major proponent and purveyor of quality.

A continual process of getting at value-based issues in your customer businesses is indispensable to staying on top of your competitive advantage. There are two time frames in which you must know your customers' needs for value, present and future. In both of them, you must know customer value needs according to their business functions as well as by their lines of business.

Asking Present-Value Questions

The single most important issue you can resolve in your current business is its degree of adaptibility and responsiveness to customer needs for value. In every industry, values constantly change. Competitive pressures force them to undergo alteration, along with parallel pressures from economic cycles, technological innovations, and global politics. It is all too easy to think you know your customers' current needs for values because you knew them last year. But if your customers' needs for value change and your response remains stagnant, you will become progressively valueless to them.

Customers should be asked periodically—the period will vary with their industry but it should never be longer than semiannually—Where are your greatest needs for value?

> "In order to remain competitively advantaged, where do you need to subtract negative worth and where do you need to add positive value—to or from which processes, which products, which of your people?"

> "Has competition revealed that your meantime between new products being developed by R&D has become overly long?"

> "Is your meantime between downtimes in manufacturing unduly short?"

> "Is market information lagging behind results?"

> "Are your current product leaders all at the same mature point in their life cycles?"

> "Is your current top management similarly mature?"

> "Where are today's most critical success factors in your business?"

> "Are they in order entry, customer service, quality control, inventory management?"

> "What is our current contribution to you in each of these areas where we are a major player?"

> "How, and by how much, must it be improved to make an advantageous impact on your competitive position?"

Asking Future-Value Questions

In many industries, "the future" is coming sooner than ever. It is running backward into the present, blurring the fine line that might otherwise unambiguously announce that "the future is now." Lest you be overtaken and underprepared, you must always be curious about future values that can be anticipated in your major markets.

While you are assessing customer needs for current values, you should ask:

"Where will your greatest needs for values be next
   year—and the next year after that?"
"What will be different about your competitive challenges and the ways you are planning to anticipate
   them?"
"What contributions will you demand from us?"
"What will the best ways be for us to make them?"

You can expect a wide range of responses, many of
which will be broad generalizations while others will be
extremely finite:

"We must have a completely automated system for forecasting, inventory, order entry, billing, and collec-
   tions."
"We must have flexible manufacturing in order to han-
   dle small production runs more cost-effectively."
"We must be able to analyze the profitability of each
   customer, each product line, and each branch in each
   region, in order to focus our marketing resources on
   the most profitable segments."
"We need to develop more rigorous profiles of good and
   poor credit risks in order to increase our rejection
   rate on a rational basis."
"We need to identify our best customers for cross-selling
   related products."
"We need to reduce the interest we are paying on borrowed funds."
"We need to make marginal customers more profitable
   by having a better method of breakeven analysis on
   small shipments."
"We need to know the optimal mix of leased and owned
   equipment, of make and buy production, of full-time
   and part-time personnel."
"We need more and better information on what is hap-
   pening in our markets and we need it faster."
"We need to be able to respond to information quicker."
"We need to make better decisions when we respond:
   Should we coupon, price off, offer two for one, or
   cross-sell?"

Making Your Value Count the Most

The three quantifiers of value—*how much, how soon,* and *how sure*—are one part of the answer to value maximization. The other part is the qualifier of value: *where to add it.* In theory, there are no wrong places in which to add value to a customer's business. All added value that meets or exceeds a customer's minimum hurdle rate and maximum payback requirements is good value, contributing to competitive advantage. Yet two answers to the question "Where?" are better than all others. If you concentrate on them, you will be able to make your value count the most because you will be putting it where each customer can maximize it.

1. *Adding value to counteract a customer's most crucial costs.* Each customer has a set of costs that contribute more to his competitive disadvantage than any other. These are the accumulated costs of his main deliverables, which include all the investments that go into researching, developing, engineering, manufacturing, and marketing the 20 percent of his products that give him up to 80 percent of his profitable sales volume.

These costs are crucial because they determine whether or not a customer can be the low-cost supplier in his industry, or at least competitive with the supplier who is, in the product categories that make the greatest contributions to his profits. If he cannot be cost-competitive in the 20 percent that yield him 80 percent, it will not matter what he does or does not do to be competitive in the 80 percent that yield only the remaining 20 percent of profits. Any value you can add to reduce or eliminate the costs contributed by his big-winning "20 percenters" will have a worth to him that is far in excess of the same or even greater values you may be able to add elsewhere in his business.

2. *Adding value to accelerate a customer's most crucial profit generators.* Each customer has one or two lines of business that contribute more to his competitive advantage than any

other. These are his "20 percenters," his maximum profit generators that can earn up to 80 percent of his total profits on sales.

The products, services, or systems in these lines of business are crucial because they determine whether or not a customer can be the high-profit supplier in his industry, or at least competitive with the supplier who is, in the businesses that make the greatest contributions to his overall profits. If he cannot maximize the earnings from these blue-chip businesses—the 20 percent that yield up to 80 percent of his profits—it will not matter what he does or does not do to maximize the profits of the rest. Any value you can add to increasing the profits contributed by his big-winning "20 percenters" will have a worth to him that is far in excess of the same or even greater values you may be able to add elsewhere in his business.

Before you can add value to his most crucial profit generators, you will have to know how he makes his profits from each of these lines of business. There are two possibilities for making your value count the most:

1. If the customer has low unit margins and therefore generates his big-winner profits primarily by *turnover,* you will have to add value to his abilities to take orders, produce, ship and deliver, and collect his receivables with the maximum cost-effectiveness.
2. If the customer has low turnover and therefore must generate his big-winner profits primarily on *margin,* you will have to add value to his capabilities to differentiate his product or, more likely, his applications, support, and service skills. In this way, he can maximize their contribution to his customers' ability to minimize their own most crucial costs or maximize their own most crucial profit generators.

In order to make your added value count the most, you must keep two guidelines in mind:

1. Whenever you propose to add value by reducing or

eliminating a customer cost, pass your proposal
through a three-question screen:
- Does it affect at least one of the customer's most
  crucial costs?
- If so, is the cost effect significant?
- If not, why bother with it?

2. Whenever you propose to add value by expanding a
   customer revenue or earnings flow, pass your pro-
   posal through a three-question screen:
   - Does it affect at least one of the customer's most
     crucial revenue generators?
   - If so, is the revenue effect significant?
   - If not, why bother with it?

All business managers strive to maximize the contributions of their most crucial revenue generators. This is their
key to profits. If you can position yourself as a value-adder
through revenue expansion, you have the best chance of
becoming a customer's strategic ally because all businesses
exist to make money. No business exists simply to reduce its
costs. Yet cost reduction is often the only way a business,
especially one that is mature, can free up funds for growth
that can be used as the equivalent of new revenues. If you
can add value only through cost reduction, you should
present the costs you release from customer operations as
equivalent revenues so you can still relate to—and be related
to—a customer's primary money-making objectives.

If you are going to make it your business, in the most
literal sense, to know your value and, by letting your customers also know your value as well as price your value and sell
your value, you may want to ask yourself one more value-
based question: Should your compensation system be predicated on paying for the performance of value creation?
Paying for value creation means rewarding your value creators in direct proportion to the quantifiable values they
create for your customers, which is, of course, the sole source
of your own value.

This will force you to think properly about value: Who
are our prime value creators? Who supports them? What are

the components of the values they create? How much value comes from saving customer costs and how much from expanding customer revenues and earnings? Among all our value-creators, who are the most cost-effective? Who are the most consistent? Who are most proficient in creating value for start-up customers, for customers who are in the high-growth phase of their life cycles, or for mature customers? Who is the best customer grower, adding to customer profits at a progressively increasing annual rate year after year as a demonstration of his or her growing mastery of the customer's business?

Compensating a sales force on the basis of the total number of units of products or service hours it sells, or on the basis of the total revenues derived from them, has always been a meaningless index of value creation. The customer's best interests, linked to his competitive advantage, have been found nowhere in the compensation equation. Value-based compensation makes the customer the paymaster. It is quid-pro-quo pay, founded squarely on the same kind of performance base that is typically used by many customers to reward their own managers. In this sense, it does not lack for precedent. Nor does it lack for its ability to remind your people that they live by the customer values they create.

Positioning Yourself on the Value Chain

In traditional business management, it was gospel that each business had to own the complete value chain in its industry. This led to horizontally integrated monoliths that made everything internally and bought as little as possible from the outside. The reasons given were always cost control and quality control, sometimes supplemented by the need for an assured supply. Yet, in reality, costs were rarely controlled. Massive and widespread cost-inefficiencies were rife but hidden from accountability by transfer-cost systems that disguised what was actually being appropriated or misappropriated, spent or misspent.

Gradually, manufacturers and processors have discovered that contract suppliers can often be more cost-effective and equally quality controlled, in addition to keeping their fixed costs off the balance sheet. When they distributed their own costs across their operations, many manufacturers also learned that they were investing more in peripheral activities than in their main businesses: Warehousing and distribution cost more for brewers, for example, than did brewing the beer itself.

The "whole earth" myth of the need to own value chains from beginning to end has been debunked. So has the myth of which end of the value chain is really the end. Value chains are now seen to begin not with manufacturing access to raw materials or a process for refining them but with consultative access to customers. Everything flows "backward" from there, because customers are the source of all value and their needs for added value must determine each preceding link in the value chains that serve them.

Many suppliers, even otherwise enlightened ones, are still stuck at the low manufacturing end of their industry's value chain. William Gates of The Microsoft Corporation speaks for this product-based point of view when he says that "consulting services are a natural extension of our personal computing offerings" rather than the other way around. As a product person, he is comfortable in touching his customers first with his software, even though it has much less value both to them and to him, rather than counselling with them on the superior values from its application to their businesses.

The supplier who is closest to the customer is number one in the value chain. He is the end applier of all preceding values and he is the one who must consult on how to package them, manage them, implement them, and make them competitively advantageous to the customer. He can be thought of as a value synthesizer or, as he is sometimes called, a systems integrator. In Figure 1-3, he is at the high end of the value chain. The farther back you go, the less value you can price and sell because the less value you can add.

The closer you come to the high end of the value chain where you can touch your end-user customer—the more you

Figure 1-3. The value chain.

		• Facilities Manager
Manufacturer	Systems Seller	• Systems Integrator
		• Category Manager
		• Value-Added Reseller

◀ Low ————————————————————— High ▶
  End   End

- Low Value
- Low Margins
- High Costs

- High Value
- High Margins
- Low Costs

know his business, the more you can affect it, and the more readily you can measure your contribution—the greater your value will be and the greater leverage you have on price. Conversely, the more remote you are from your end-user customers at the low end of Figure 1-3, the lower the value you will have to sell and the lower its price will be.

From left to right, the value chain is a continuum of the ability to contribute competitive advantage. It is also a margin continuum, because margins track value. From right to left, the value chain is a cost continuum. The low end of the value chain is typically where the high end of costs accumulate, most of them sunk into plant and equipment and other fixed capital expenses. Toward the high end of the value chain, costs become lighter and more variable because they are largely people costs.

People-intensive businesses are greater value-adders than capital-intensive businesses because it takes consultative people to apply capital and train other people to extract its full value in partnership with them. Furthermore, people are expected to be innovative whereas capital equipment is expected to be standardized in conformity to customer-prescribed "open standards" that conspire against proprietary capabilities.

The first principle of selling must be to price your

greatest value, not your greatest cost. A manufacturer's greatest value is never found in his physical product. That is where his costs are concentrated. If he bases price on his product, he will receive margins proportional to his costs, not his value. This is a recipe for competitive disadvantage.

Businesses at the high end of the value chain that manage a customer's internal operating facilities, that integrate the products of multiple vendors into coherent systems, and that consult on adding value by application and implementation have the right recipe for competitive advantage. They can maximize value to the customer. By contrast, businesses at the value chain's low end have only "box value" and the capability of their "hardware" and perhaps also their supportive "software" to affect price. The price they can hold out will be cost-based. If they compete box to box with other businesses, the low-margin seller will win. If they sell to multivendor systems integrators or through third-party "value-added resellers," they will pay a similar price in margin.

Wherever you are on the value chain, you are in danger if you do not know your value. Try as you may to protect them, your margins will always be indecently exposed. Leads will evade you or, when you find them, they may very well embarrass you, as the following scenario shows.

A test and measurement equipment supplier learned that the maintenance cost of a customer's calibration process averaged 5 percent of the cost of each of his products that passed through it. "We can reduce that," he said. "To what?" he was asked. "Oh, let's say 3 percent," he answered. Later, he discovered that the industry average was 6 to 8 percent and that his own company's historical norms ranged from 10 to 12 percent.

"Well, then," he said, "let us look at your labor costs. At 66 percent of total maintenance costs, they appear to be much too high." But they turned out to be among the lowest in the customer's industry and had been going down each year. "Let us pull the overtime costs out of total labor cost," the supplier suggested next. But overtime accounted for only 3 percent of all labor cost against an industry average of 6 percent.

There was nothing left to say to the customer except "Congratulations." Glances were traded, but no money. Money changes hands only when customers congratulate their suppliers.

2

Know Your Value

When you compete on value, you must know each major customer's cost problems and revenue opportunities. Cost problems represent negative values. They need to be avoided, reduced, or eliminated altogether. Revenue opportunities represent positive values. They need to be taken advantage of faster, less expensively, more successfully, and at higher margins. You need to know three things about them:

1. Know the customer's critical cost factors and critical revenue-expansion or margin factors.
2. Know the current negative values of each cost factor and the current positive values of each revenue and margin factor.
3. Know the customer's objectives to reduce each cost factor and expand each revenue and margin factor.

In this context, knowing your own business takes on new meanings:

- Knowing your norms for reducing the customer's negative values and expanding his positive values.
- Knowing how much value you can bring to each negative value to reduce it and how much value you can

add to each positive value to expand it. These values will become your "product line."

If, for example, your competitive position is going to be based on adding value to brand managers of consumer packaged-goods businesses, you must help them add to one or more of their value-based objectives:

- Meet volume goals.
- Meet margin targets.
- Achieve market share.
- Make payback for new products on plan.
- Maximize the conversion rate of first-time tryers to repeat purchasers.
- Maximize the return on promotional investments.
- Maximize the number of orders filled on time.
- Minimize per-unit sales costs.

If your competitive position is going to be based on adding value to manufacturing managers of industrial businesses, you must help them add value to a different set of objectives:

- Maximize uptime and minimize downtime.
- Maximize on-spec production as close as possible to zero defects to minimize reject rates and scrap.
- Minimize the cost contributions of labor, materials, and energy.
- Minimize changeover cycles.

Opening Your Consciousness to Value

Insofar as you do not know any of the values you contribute to your customers, you will commit yourself to being competitively disadvantaged. You must know the customer business functions and lines of business to which you add value. You must know their managers' objectives that you must enhance. You must know how much value you can add and how soon your customers can most likely achieve it. You must know how certain they can be that the value you promise them will be the value that actually accrues. This means that you must become expert in knowing how you add value and how much value you add: in other words what critical success factors you affect in customer functions and businesses and how much you affect them.

The computer industry shows the transcendent power of competing on value. In an industry filled with product-obsessed vendors who annually sell more and more performance at less and less price, IBM was for many years the only consultant. It sold on value. As a result, its values became the industry standards of most of its major customers. Several of its competitors could probably have produced higher values, and were quite likely doing so, but it never occurred to them to find out or to sell on them. Hewlett-Packard Company was one of these technology-driven competitors that defined itself as "a vendor of manufacturing systems" and was content to "finish in the top two or three survivors" when it went up against IBM. Customers began to accept HP as a second or third source and, in that role, many customers assumed that no matter what the company said it could do, IBM could probably do it better. Whenever HP sold, it risked making a market for IBM.

You can get to know your value through a two-step process. First, you must translate your product or service features into their performance benefits. This will give you their *operating values*. Then you must translate the performance benefits into *financial values*. This will give you the costs you can help save, avoid, or offset by revenues, or it will give you the revenues themselves that you can increase. These economic results are your real values. They form your true product specifications and create the only meaningful competitive definition of your business.

Value competition requires an accurate, consistent computation of your impacts on the customer operations that you affect. How much profit is being added? How soon has it begun to flow? How long before it fully accumulates?

There are three types of values that you must know

about your business. Some of them will be *restorative*. They will restore insufficient values being generated by your customers due to unnecessarily excessive costs or correctible problems in their productivity. Other values will be *opportunistic* in the sense of enabling your customers to seize sales opportunities that would otherwise remain beyond their reach or increase the opportunity for them to earn higher margins on their current sales. A third type of values will be *preventive*.

Values that can prevent a customer from incurring a competitive disadvantage are priceless. No business can afford even a temporary disadvantage in either unnecessary costs incurred by its operations or in the opportunity costs of failing to fully commercialize one of its major markets. Failures that are not prevented must be corrected after the fact. At that stage, proposed remedies are expensive. They may not work. Even if they do work, it may be too late to regain a lost competitive advantage.

When you know what your value is worth to a customer, you and your customer can tell what kind of "partner material" you represent. If, working alone without you, the customer can obtain the same value as he would get from working with you, you will not be partner material. If your value is worth more than what the customer can obtain working alone or with any other supplier, you will be prime partner material.

If you want to be prime partner material, you must offer a prime value. Nobody must be able to offer the customer a better mix of value specifications, either as much value or as soon or as sure, depending on his needs. If you can achieve this position with your major customers, you will have a new basis for your price. No longer will your price need to reflect your costs or be constrained by competitive prices. You will be able to relate your price to the worth of your value on a return-on-investment basis. This is the way that value-based pricing can transcend competitive bidding. When competition is no longer the index of price, the criterion of "fair price" shifts to customer value. All other bases for price become noncompetitive.

Being the High-Value Partner

Partnering is based on value. To the extent that you add
value, you add to your partnerability. "Making partner"
means making the highest value impact on your customers'
competitiveness.

If you want to maximize your business growth, you will
have to choose between two courses of action. One is to
become the low-cost supplier in your industry and to pass
your cost advantages along to your customers in the form of
low prices. These will help make your customers lower-cost
producers themselves. They will then have the same option
you have to pass cost savings along to their own customers.
Together, you and your customers—and presumably your
suppliers as well, because you will make sure that they pass
low costs along to you—will form a value network based on
price.

Everywhere in the network, prices will be low. So will
investment in R&D, services, and marketing. The margins to
support them will be nonexistent. Growth throughout the
network will depend on volume, not margins. The prime
requirement to be a low-cost supplier will be the ability to
ride the learning curves of mass production and mass marketing.

The other course of action to maximize your business
growth is to become the high-value partner in your industry
and to pass your value along to your customers in return for
high margins. The value you add can help make your customers lower-cost producers themselves or high-value, high-
margin marketers. Together, you and your customers will
form a network based on value.

Everywhere in the network, margins will be high. So will
investment in customer service, especially application, implementation and installation, education, information, and consultation. Growth throughout the network will depend on
margins multiplied by cost-effective volume.

Low-cost businesses and high-value businesses can both
be successfully run. It is hybridization that causes problems

because there is no middle ground for a third type. A low-cost supplier that tries to compete on customer services will go broke. Similarly, so will a high-value supplier that tries to match prices with a low-cost competitor. Each must play its own game.

Unfortunately, low-cost suppliers will not let high-value competitors play a high-value game. The ceaseless quest of low-cost suppliers for more and more volume to support their low costs forces them to penetrate the markets of high-value suppliers. From the bottom of each customer base, they carve niches where susceptibility to price appeals is great. As soon as high-value suppliers take the bait and respond by sympathetically reducing their prices, their high profits are doomed.

Value—its controlled maintenance, its predictable reliability, and its continuous innovation—is the only defense. The correct reaction to lower price must be greater value or more quickly realized value or more certain value, not a matching lower price. The proper response to low-cost competition is better application, better implementation and installation, better education, and better information and consultation. If you cannot grow a business as a high-value supplier under these conditions, you will never make it as a high-value supplier who tries to sell at a low-cost supplier's prices.

Assessing Your Value

Unquantified value is unmarketable value. If you cannot put a number on the value you represent, you cannot price it or sell it. Yet this does not deter many managers from trying. They attempt to sell "hidden value," the business equivalent of the cat in a bag, either by surmise or surprise.

If you ask a customer to surmise your value, you ask him to make a guess about something that he may not know at all. As a result, customers play it safe. If you try to assure a customer that your value is "in there" without specifying its muchness, soonness, or sureness, he will underestimate it.

When he downsizes his perception of your value, he will also downsize his acceptance of your premium price. Every time you tell him that your value is "more than you think," he will cut back on your margins more than you like.

Hidden value that has the power to surprise a customer also presents a marketing problem. Customers learn, most of them the hard way, that there is no such thing in business as a good surprise. They want their businesses to proceed according to plan. Surprise is something to be engineered out of plans, not invited into them. When a surprise occurs, it is automatically regarded as an aberration, a signal that something has gone wrong. Your value must always be in your popcorn—your product—and never in the surprise hidden in the box.

Even if your value is small, it can still have an important impact. You can compete on value even if you can only improve the competitiveness of a customer operation at the level of one: For example, one hour saved each day in a customer's business function or one dollar of profit gained with each sale in a line of business can have significant meaning in any competitive industry. Value-based what-ifs like these can become your sales strategy:

- What if you can reduce the length of your sales cycle or collection cycle or order-fulfillment cycle or design cycle by as little as one day? How many dollars of cost will that save and how many new dollars of revenues will that earn?
- What if you can add the equivalent of one more hour of productive output to each shift's work cycle or the equivalent of one more work shift each month without additional cost? How many new dollars of revenue will that earn for you?
- What if you can add just one more penny to your margins on each sale or one more percent to your market share? How many new dollars of revenues and earnings will you gain?

Value assessment calculates the contributions you have already made to customer competitive advantage. It also provides the measurement system that will enable you to prove your present contributions. A standard process for measuring your value is every bit as important as standard processes for creating value. If you are a value-adder, you are required, of necessity, to be a value measurer; otherwise you risk having your contributions go unknown and unrewarded. Either your customers will be ignorant of your values or they will incorrectly perceive someone else to be the value leader. Suppose that the contribution you can make to a customer's profit improvement normally averages $3 million over the first three years. If you do not know it and a competitor represents his norm at $1.5 million, he will become the industry standard because you cannot prove your higher value. You will lose by default.

Suppose that your normal contribution of $3 million in expanded revenues can be earned at an average reduced sales cost of $2 million and that there are $350,000 in additional labor savings available along with $500,000 in saved materials and processing costs. If you do not know these values, you will lose to a competitor who may be able to match or exceed your revenue expansion norm but not your savings.

Suppose a major customer challenges you with a competitor's values: "We have been approached by another supplier in your industry with the following offer: He proposes to add between $3 and $6 million in annual revenues and another $300,000 to $600,000 in reduced costs to our marketing operations, with the added values starting to flow after the first ninety days. What can you do for us in these areas?

"Your competitor has identified one of our marketing functions as capable of contributing the majority of our improved revenues and reduced costs. Which function do you normally concentrate on? What is its normal contribution to new earnings and savings?"

When you know your value, you have the answers.

Formulating an Assessment Process

Value assessment is designed to accomplish two objectives. One is to assess your *previously contributed values* that form the basis for your norms. Norms represent the historical aggregate of your values and summarize your track record as a value-adder. Second, value assessment is designed to assess your *future opportunity to contribute value* based on applying your norms to current customer values.

The BSI-Wellspring method, which is the proprietary assessment strategy of Business Science International and of The Wellspring Group, measures customer value at each point of contribution: the work of groups of "value owners" that operate the critical success factors in each critical success function or critical success business.

Value owners are the "critical few" managers in a business. They are the 20 percenters—the managers who control the critical success factors in the most critical success business functions and lines of business. No matter how many men and women a business employs, the small band of value owners "own" the business. They hold its competitive advantage in their hands.

The following examples will give you an idea of who the value owners are in the customer business you sell to:

- For a consumer packaged goods manufacturer, brand managers are a critical work group of value owners. Competitive sales analysis is one of their critical success factors. Another work group of value owners operates the critical success factor of order entry in the critical success function of inventory management.

- For an industrial or technical systems manufacturer, researchers and developers are a critical work group of value owners. New-product modeling and design is one of their critical success factors. Another work group of value owners operates the critical success factor of on-line quality control in the critical success function of computer-aided manufacturing.

- For a professional services business, marketers are a critical work group of value owners. Market segmentation is one of their critical success factors. Another work group of value owners operates the critical success factor of compensation policy planning in the critical success function of human resources management.

In order to assess the current values being realized by each work group of value owners, the BSI-Wellspring method uses an assessment process that has the following five characteristics:

1. It is industry specific.
2. Within each industry, it is business specific.
3. Within each business, it is specific to a critical success business function.
4. Within each business function, it is specific to a critical success factor.
5. Within each critical success factor, it is specific to its work group.

Figure 2-1 identifies some typical work groups of value owners.

Setting Assessment Objectives

Your value assessment process should be able to accomplish two things:

1. Develop leads for new sales based on the assessment of current customer values that are inferior to your norms so that you can propose adding your values to them.
2. Teach you the actual values you deliver on each proposal by measuring how much your customers realize as a result of your contributions and how soon they realize it.

Figure 2-1. Work groups of value owners and their critical
success functions.

Critical Success Functions	Value Owners
Research and Development	New Product Designers
	New Materials Researchers
	New Process Developers
Manufacturing	Production Planners
	Quality Controllers
Sales and Distribution	Order Enterers
	Inventory Controllers
Finance	Credit Issuers and Collectors
	Account Payers
Marketing	Advertising Managers and Teams
	Market Researchers
Management Information Services (MIS)	Data Processors

In order to achieve these objectives, value assessment
should become an integral part of every major sale you make.
To sell and remain ignorant of the value you have contributed is to make only one-third of a sale, the money part. The
other two-thirds are composed of the knowledge part, that
is, knowing each contribution you make to customer value
and being able to average it into your norms; and the next-
lead part, that is, using your value as a starting point for
adding new values from follow-on sales.

Selling and assessing the customer value of the sale are
part and parcel of a single transaction. "We sell value," value-
based suppliers say to their customers. "As a result, we
measure what we sell: How much value do we actually deliver
and how soon? We would like you to partner with us in our
assessment process so that we can learn together how to keep
improving the contributions we make to your competitive
advantage and to take immediate remedial action if our

contribution should go off plan or if your competitive situation changes."

If you think of your value assessment process as the prime lead generator for future sales, you will never sell without it. It has become a business platitude to say that no sale is complete until the customer is satisfied. But how can you know: simply by an absence of complaints or the continuing flow of orders at the normal level? You must be aggressive about customer satisfaction, making sure that you know, and that your customers know along with you, exactly what values you are adding to them. A continuous, mandatory value assessment program in partnership with each major customer is the only way you can be sure of receiving proper credit for your contribution so that you get the full value out of your value.

Managing Basic Assessment Procedures

A value assessment process requires three things:

1. A set of *benchmark measurements* of the current customer values to be improved: This is the "before."
2. A series of *milestone measurements* while your value-adding application or installation is in progress: This is the "during."
3. A *final measurement* of the total values that have been contributed and an assessment of the potential future values that can be added: This is the "after."

Benchmark measurements mark the starting point for adding value. They define the current performance of a customer's critical success function or critical success business. In the case of a cost-centered function, you will want to benchmark two things: the function's current contribution to total customer costs and, within it, the contributions that each critical success factor is making to total function costs. In the case of a profit-centered business, you will want to benchmark two different things: the business line's current contribution to total customer revenues and earnings and, within it, the contributions that each critical success factor is making to total business revenues and earnings. Figure 2-2 shows how this works.

You will need to benchmark two sets of performance values. One set is *financial,* expressed as dollars and percentages of current contribution of either costs or revenues and earnings. The second set is composed of the *operating* values that contribute the costs or revenues and earnings. For a business function, these will normally include labor intensity; the cycle times for design, manufacture, order fulfillment, and receivables collection; and the meantimes between downtime, new product introductions, and reorders. For a line of business, operating values to be benchmarked will normally include customer satisfaction ratings, market share, the meantime between competitive action and response, stockout and backorder rates, and the cycle time and cost required to make major sales.

Once benchmarks have been established, *milestone measurements* must be made to mark the periodic progress from "before" to "after." Their frequency will depend on the total cycle time for each value-adding project and where the project is at any given time in its cycle. For example, a project that is proposed to pay back its investment by month 3 should be milestoned with greater frequency than a project with a longer payback, for instance a month 9 deadline. All projects should be milestoned more frequently in their early stages to make sure they are on track. They should also be milestoned more frequently near the end, when full payout is close at hand, in order to make certain that the proposed net values are going to be fully delivered.

In addition to learning how much value you contribute on a milestone-by-milestone basis, progress measurements teach you how soon your values accrue. From your milestones, you will learn how soon your customers' paybacks normally occur so that they are made financially whole again, how soon customer cash flows normally turn from negative to positive, and how soon customers can normally expect to receive the full return of value from their investments with

Figure 2-2. Benchmarking scheme.

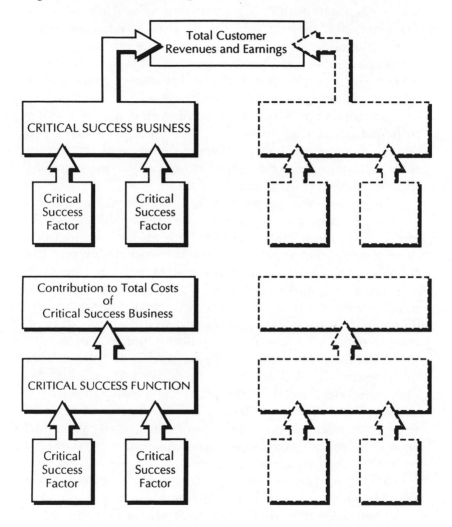

you. In addition to these financial values, you will also learn how soon their underlying operating values are normally delivered: how soon labor intensity is reduced, how soon a newly trained work group can resume its normal levels of productivity and then begin to exceed them, and how soon market share responds to improved inventory management or cents-off or two-for-one promotions.

Another benefit of milestoning is that it serves as the principal partnering strategy of the value assessment process. When you and your customers milestone together, you both learn how customer operations can be managed for their maximum contributions to value.

Your *final measurements* in value assessment are to learn how much value you can contribute. While they mark the end point to your assessment of each project to add value, they provide the platform for each successive project that follows. One project's final measurement is the next project's opening benchmark. Now that you have added value, how much more can you add? What new opportunities have been discovered? Where else can you add value? What old problems remain? What more can you add to improve them?

Final measurements are the wellspring of your marketing strategy. From them, you can derive the case histories that prove your ability to contribute as a value-adder, testimonials from your customers who have benefited competitively from your values, and the norms that certify your track record as prime partner material and industry standard-bearer for the values you represent.

When you set out on your first value assessment, you should expect to encounter one or more cases of "value surprise." Your attention will almost always be called to an added value you did not expect, a cost or revenue benefit that has been enjoyed by a customer business function manager or line manager whose participation in your value chain has been unknown to you. No matter how well you know your customer businesses, there is usually at least one obscure beneficiary of your value whose rewards are significant but whose contribution to your track record, and hence to your norms, has been zero. As you come upon these beneficiaries, your value surprises can be added to your claims of a competitive edge.

Valuing Critical Success Factors

Knowing your value enables you to capture the market for one or more critical success factors. If you know your values in helping customers apply a just-in-time inventory strategy, for example, you may be able to capture the market for adding savings and revenue values to one or more of their critical success factors for inventory:

- They will be able to save costs of inventory storage and handling charges, insurance, security and warehousing facilities, the opportunity losses from cash that would otherwise be tied up in inventory, and the direct costs of borrowing that are often made necessary by tied-up funds.
- They will be able to make money by improving productivity, adjust their product mix more readily to demand, and move more products on time through their distribution channels. On-time delivery is a critical success factor. An improvement in delivery time from 96 percent to 97 percent for a consumer packaged goods manufacturer can add $50 million to $80 million in revenues to his retail customers.

If you know your values in helping customers enter new products in their markets ahead of plan, you may be able to capture the market for adding savings and revenue values to one or more of their critical success factors for new products:

- They will be able to save design and development costs and release their development people earlier from each project to get to work on the next project.
- They will be able to make money by getting to market first, establish a leadership position, and fill their dis-

tribution channels to create earlier positive cash flow and a preemptive market share.

If you know your values in helping customers improve their planning of product-by-product, market-by-market, region-by-region sales, you may be able to capture the market for adding savings and revenue values to one or more of their critical success factors for sales:

- They will be able to save money by discontinuing cost-ineffective promotions earlier, counteract competitive price and promotion strategies faster, and allocate expenditures more accurately to growth products, markets, and regions.
- They will be able to make money by correcting price disparities, capitalize sooner on successful new products by supporting them vigorously, and correct out-of-stock conditions to assure sales.

In each of these cases, you will be selecting a customer whose business you believe you can grow and focusing on one of his critical success functions or critical success businesses—the "20 percenters" that account for up to 80 percent of his costs or revenues and earnings. Within each function or business, you will be targeting a critical success factor that is itself a "20 percenter" in terms of the contribution it makes to the competitive advantage of its function or business. In this way, you will always be adding value to customers where they need it the most, where they can afford it the most, and where they will be able to see the most impressive results from it on their top or bottom lines.

Measuring Value by Customer Satisfaction

Customer satisfaction is the ultimate measure of value because it is the only customer-driven measurement. All other criteria of value are subjective: your quality, your reliability, or your response to problems and how quickly and competently you resolve them. Value is the cause of customer satisfaction. When John Akers, chairman of IBM, says that "We measure all IBMers on their contribution to customer satisfaction," he is saying that his people are measured by IBM according to the customer value they add . . . the same way they are measured by their customers.

In value terms, a "satisfied customer" is one who is receiving the added value he needs when he needs it, not simply purchasing added products or services. A "satisfactory supplier" is one who is giving him the added value by means of one or both of two strategies:

1. The supplier is making or saving the maximum amount of value for his customer and it is more value than the customer can add to his own business by himself or from a competitive supplier at comparable levels of investment and risk.
2. The supplier is costing the minimum amount of value for his customer by minimizing hidden costs, indirect costs, recurrent life-cycle costs, and all expenditures that the customer must budget as unrecoverable costs instead of returnable investments.

Customer satisfaction comes from adding value to a customer's critical success functions or critical success businesses. Within each function or business, a customer depends on a small "must list" of values. Unless the contribution of the "must list" to his profits can be maximized, he risks competitive disadvantage. Some of the "musts" are related to your products; others are related to your services. Altogether, seven values are crucial:

Product-Related Values

1. Value-to-price relationship
2. Product quality
3. Product benefits and features
4. Reliability

Service-Related Values

5. Training
6. Warranty
7. Repair and replacement

Taken as a group, these seven values determine your ability to add satisfactorily to a customer's profits by reducing his costs or increasing his revenues and earnings. Without enhancing these values, you will be less than satisfactory or unsatisfactory as a supplier. Your customer's costs will not be reduced enough or quickly enough or the expansion of his revenues and earnings according to his plans will remain unrealized.

Value assessment and customer satisfaction go hand in hand. When you assess your value to each customer, you should ask questions like these:

- What are the current costs we are contributing to the critical success functions that determine our customer's competitive advantage as a low-cost supplier?
- What are the current revenues and earnings we are contributing to the critical success businesses that determine our customer's competitive advantage as a profit leader or market-share leader?
- How do these values compare against our customer's "must list"?
- How do these values compare against our competitors' values?

The direct interrelationship between added value and customer satisfaction shows up clearly when the basis for satisfaction is examined so that the contribution made by value can be separately quantified. A typical finding is summarized in Figure 2-3.

When only one supplier sells value, he dominates satisfaction. When no supplier sells value, purchase decisions are thrown back onto performance benefits. Because there is

Figure 2-3. The value/customer-satisfaction relationship.

	High Satisfaction (%)	Low or No Satisfaction (%)
When you sell value	73	0
When you do not sell value but a competitor does	0	76
When neither of you sells value	36	29

little performance differentiation, the result is little difference in satisfaction.

Proposing What's in It for Your Customers

Your value to your customers is their incremental gain from doing business with you. Beyond the products, equipment, and systems they acquire—which, except for their depreciation, represent negative values as costs—they seek to add value to their operations in order to gain, maintain, or regain competitive advantage. What are they getting for their money? If all they know is their cost of doing business with you, that is, how much they spend, they will never know what value you bring them.

All customer decision making is based on differential analysis. Is a deal a good one? There is no way to tell without knowing its value. Then it can be compared against two standards. One is the hurdle rate that establishes the minimal values required from incremental investments. The other is the range of values offered at the same time by competitive opportunities to invest similar amounts of funds at similar levels of risk. Under these two standards of comparison, the answers to five questions can be evaluated:

1. Which deal offers the biggest payout?
2. Which deal offers the quickest payback?

3. Which deal is the surest bet?
4. Are there better deals offered by other investments?
5. Should we simply pull out of the "deal market" and bank our money until a truly worthwhile deal comes along?

By comparing different opportunities to invest their money, customers decide whether or not to do business with any other supplier in your business category. What is the most likely value of an automated information system, for example, or of a pollution control system or a resource recovery system or an electronic mail system? At this point, it makes no difference whose system it may be; customers ask only, Is there value here for us?

Second, is it a greater value than its alternatives?

Only if a customer gets a *yes* answer to both questions in your category of business will your competitive value come into play. This will determine whether you will be the supplier of choice; in other words, the customer's preferred value-adder. Unless your customers know the standard values that your solutions can provide—in other words, *your normative values*—they will not be able to realize that improvements over their current values are available to them. Unless they know the specific value that you can add to their problem or opportunity—in other words, *your proposed value*—they will not be able to fund you. They will have no idea of what they are being asked to buy.

As a result, they may invest their funds for a lower return somewhere else or with one of your competitors instead of you. They may lose value, suffering opportunity loss if the value that you represent could have given them a greater or earlier or more certain competitive advantage. In their best interest, to say nothing of your own, you cannot afford to let this happen. If you do and a customer were to become competitively disadvantaged, his prospectiveness would be diminished as a source of growth for you. His growth would have been impaired, making him a poorer partner for you because he would be less able to sponsor your own growth. This would be your just return, or course, for failing to sponsor his growth by allowing him to remain, along with you, ignorant of your potential added value.

If you sell a technology-based product or process, it is imperative that your customers' general managers—the controllers and allocators of customer funds—know its value. Your value must permeate their decision making at the divisional, department, and operating levels that include their major cost-centered business functions and strategic business units. They may not understand your technology nor may they care to or need to. But they understand value.

A flexible manufacturing system or computer-aided design process supported by artificial intelligence may be a thing of beauty to you and you may feel comfortable referring to it as an FMS or CAD supported by AI. But beauty of this kind is only in your own eyes. Top- and middle-level customer managers find their beauty in beholding value—in the returns on their investments, not the investments themselves. Your FMS is their ROI, the return on investing in it. Your CAD is their NPV, the net present value of three years of improved cash flows as a result of owning and operating a flexible manufacturing system or designing their new products by computer.

If you represent yourself to them in terms of your technologies, they will position you as a vendor and see to it that your product performance is purchased, if at all, on price. On the other hand, if you sell your value, you will be fitting yourself into the basic equation that they use to determine their competitive advantage: What will we get back for what we put out, when will we get it, and how sure can we be?

Assessing Values on and off the Bottom Line

If the values you add can reduce a business function's costs, your contribution can drop almost dollar for dollar to its bottom line: the contribution it makes to the customer's total cost. Revenue values are different. If you increase the turnover of a product line or help get a customer's new products to market faster or open up a new market for him or if your own new products help him improve his market penetration, you may have to look to find your contribution on the business unit's top line.

Your incremental values show up on the top or bottom lines of the business-function or business-line managers you work with. They are the "customers" for your values. In companies of any significant size, this is as far as you will be able to track most of them. A $1 million contribution to a line of business constitutes an important value to the line of business. It will be noticeable. But when it is passed along to a parent company in the multi-billion dollar range, you will never find it on the corporate bottom line. Unless you are affecting one of the central business functions of a customer-as-a-whole, such as corporate communications, your customer will never be the entire corporation but the specific business unit or function to which you contribute.

Business units and functional operations pay off, and their managers are paid up, on their own top and bottom line performances: How much earnings has a business unit's manager extracted from revenues? How much revenue has he or she extracted from each dollar of investment? How little cost is the manager passing along? These are the categories where you must account for your contributions.

There are three additional types of value impacts that are worthwhile for you to try to quantify in the business functions and lines of business that you affect:

1. Added *performance values* that enable customer managers to make more and better decisions faster and thereby improve their cost-effectiveness and productivity
2. Added *time values* that enable customer managers and workers to add incremental "free" minutes of availability to each hour and "free" hours to each week
3. Added *opportunity values* based on asking "What if *not*" questions that reveal the probable negative consequences of an action that is prevented from being taken or a decision that is allowed to go unmade

Without credible numbers to assess their worth, these potential values will remain mythical: perceived but inaccessible to quantification on either a top or bottom line and therefore remaining only alleged values. They are often the cause of measurable values but, in and of themselves, defy hard-nosed business justification. As long as they remain a no-man's-land of assumption and contention, your contributions to them will go without credit or compensation. For your customers, they will be similarly overlooked as competitive advantages even though they may at times be just as valuable as other, more readily measurable contributions.

Acknowledging the Ephemeral Value of Soft Values

The first rule for measuring value is "Measure what is measurable." Eliminated or reduced costs are the easiest values to measure. Increased revenues and earnings are also easy to measure. Many operating values like those shown in Figure 2-4 are readily subject to measurement. On the other hand, avoided costs and opportunity costs from lost sales are much more difficult.

Readily measurable values, which are also known as hard values, are values that can be quantified to the mutual satisfaction of you and your customers. Their ability to be quantified proves them; your agreement on their accuracy makes them acceptable as the basis for a sale. You know what you are pricing and selling. Your customers know what they are investing in and what return they can safely plan on as a result.

Some sellers try to make customers believe that there are three kinds of measurable values. The first they call "dollar values," such as lowered costs and increased revenues. The second they call "effectiveness benefits," such as increased productivity. The third they call "added-value benefits," such as improved quality of work and employee self-esteem.

Figure 2-4. Value measurability.

Readily Measurable Values	Hard-to-Measure Values
• Meantime between new product introductions	• Time saved
• Time and cost of product development cycle	• Quality improved
• Forecast accuracy compared to actual results	• Productivity gained
• Inventory costs	• Capability enhanced
• Process scheduling accuracy compared to actual results	• Motivation increased
• Speed of order entry	• Communication speeded
• Meantime between billing and collections	• Information learned
• Receivables outstanding	
• Reject and scrap rates	
• Downtime rates	
• Meantime between downtimes	
• Product movement from warehouses	
• Product movement at retail	

All three alleged kinds of value turn out to be quantifiable to one extent or another, making them all "dollar values." But only the so-called dollar values are real. If you have them on your side, you will have no need for any other kind. If you do not have them, no other kind of values will make up for them. Only dollar values are dependably "effective" and can give you justifiable self-esteem.

An inventory of hard values is necessary to keep you competitive. If your values are superior, you can be your industry leader. They are the steak and potatoes, the main course, of your sales menu because they are feedstock for your norms. The phrase "hard-value norms" is needlessly repetitive. There are no other kind.

Some businesses that are out of steak and potatoes, or are unsure of their quality, surround them or substitute for them with the parsley of "soft values." Unquantified, and in many cases unquantifiable, soft values attempt to appeal to a customer's reasonableness instead of his reason. They invite a customer to perceive what he cannot prove, asking him to accept "as reasonable" the allegation that there is a value in what the supplier is selling even though none of the specifications of value can be vouched for: neither how much nor how soon nor how sure.

In such a situation, the seller's sales strategy is to induce a customer to acknowledge that he perceives the possibility or probability of receiving a value from the seller. "Yes," a customer will be encouraged to say, "I can perceive a potential value from increasing my people's productivity." Or, "I agree that there is probably a value in motivating my work force, or increasing the amount of time that each of my sales representatives can stand before his customers, or providing my managers with more information on which to base decisions." Such perceptions are a paradox. They are often accurate, for there is some foundation of fact in them. But they are meaningless as foundations for premium pricing, which is the payoff for value-based sales.

Productivity offers a typical example of a hard-to-measure value. Many alleged increases in productivity have putative value but they cannot be readily measured. Other increases in productivity can be measured easily but turn out to have no value. This highlights the need to define each of these hard-to-measure categories with exquisite care and to ask the right questions about them:

- Whose "productivity" will be increased?
- By how much will "productivity" be increased—by enough to return or exceed the investment to increase it or by enough to significantly improve the customer's competitive advantage?
- How soon will "productivity" be increased—soon enough to pay back the investment within the customer's patience period or not soon enough?
- How sure can the customer be that "productivity" will be increased enough and on time—pretty sure or

more or less sure or will he be told that nothing in life is sure but death and taxes?

It is easy to perceive that a motivated work force will produce more work, better work, and faster work. But how much more, how much better, and how much faster? A sales representative who can stand longer and more frequently before customers can be perceived to sell more. But how much more? What will the rate of return be on the investment that frees up his nonselling time, enabling him to sell more? A manager who has access to more information to support decisions may be able to make better decisions or make more decisions faster. But how much more, how much better, and how much faster? It can be perceived equally well that more information could slow down the decision-making process.

The soft values that are produced by a customer's perceptions are, in the true sense of the word, valueless. They disdain or defy valuation. Even though they may be credited with "some value," that means only that they are worth some price.

If you do not know your value and cannot sell it, you will have to sell soft values if you want to sell value at all. This will make you an auctioneer. "What am I bid for your perception of my value?" you will be asking your customers at each value auction you conduct. This delegates control over whatever value you have to your customers. Along with it will go your margin control. Because whoever controls your margins controls your business, your customers will be running you.

There is always the chance that your customers will perceive greater value than you actually contribute and, as a result, offer you an inflated price. But there is a far more certain likelihood that they will perceive less value. In their attempt to be sure, they will discount their perceptions so that they will be able to content themselves that "some value" is not enough value or it is not deliverable soon enough or not reliable enough as a basis for your price. In the course of discounting their perceptions of your value, they will be teaching you the golden rule of value management:

If you sell values that are hard, and that have been earned and learned the hard way, soft values are meaningless. You do not need them. If you have only soft values to sell, they will also be virtually meaningless. The value of soft values, ephemeral at best, will generally be nil.

"Norming" Your Values

Norms are your aggregated added values. They tell your customers what values you are normally able to add to the contributions made by critical success factors in their critical business functions or business units. They tell *how much* value you can normally add and *how soon* it normally begins to be realized. They provide the only way you can sell the sureness of your ability as a value-adder.

Norms speak for certainty because they summarize your track record as a value-adder. If you are the best value-adder in your industry, your norms will be the industry standard—the ones to beat. As the industry standard-bearer, you can say to your competitors, "Beat us or beat it." You can say something else to your customers: "Let us show you our norms. Compare them with your current performance. If our norms represent a greater value than you are receiving right now from your operations, ask us how we can work together to bring your norms closer to ours."

Bringing customers closer to the values represented by your norms is what your competitive advantage should be based on. If you adopt this point of view, selling will become a "norm challenge." You will be able to sell by challenging customers to choose between two competitive situations: remaining at the levels of their current norms or, more advantageously, adding the value of your improved norms.

In effect, your norms serve as if-then models. They say to your customers, *If* you adopt our norms *then* you will benefit to this extent and within this time by this added value. If, for example, you adopt our norm for downtime contribution to your total manufacturing costs, then you can add $1 to $2 million a year from reduced costs. If you computerize your product testing, then you will be able to add $1.9 million to $3.5 million a year from scrap reduction. If you use our inventory management plan, then you can add between $350,000 and $500,000 a year by avoiding stockouts of your big-winner products.

When you sell value according to your norms, your "compelling selling question" changes. No longer do you have to ask, Do you want to buy our product? Nor do you have to ask, Do you want our solution? All you need to ask is: Do you want the competitive values added by our norms? If the customer says yes, you will be able to move your solution automatically into his operations.

The following two examples illustrate the norm challenge in action:

1. As a result of assessing his additive contribution to customer value, a computer manufacturer is able to issue this norm challenge to an industrial customer:

> Our customers are achieving a net profit-improvement contribution directly attributed to our systems of an average $6.3 million per year, the equivalent of 0.5 percent of their gross sales revenues, by year 2 after installation. This means that they are receiving more than a 4-to-1 rate of returned value on their investment, including their direct internal costs. By year 3, our norms show that their net profit-improvement contribution rises to an average $8.7 million, the equivalent of 0.6 percent of their gross sales revenue.

The manufacturer is then able to follow through with this partnering proposal:

> What if we can partner together to achieve similar values for you? How significant would that be in adding to your competitive advantage?

2. A professional services organization is able to issue another type of norm challenge to a consumer packaged goods (CPG) customer:

As a CPG manufacturer with a minimum of $80 million in annual turnover and at least $10 million in total promotion expenditures, our norms show that you can expect an improvement of a minimum of $1 million in promotion effectiveness within one to three years. An average of $300,000 of that amount normally accrues within year 1, paying back almost 50 percent of the total investment to achieve it within the first twelve months. These improvements are 90 percent the result of increased revenues and 10 percent the result of reduced costs.

In order to achieve improvements like these in your business, we will need to partner with the following people:

- A top-level sponsor at the VP marketing level
- A financial officer
- A data manager with access to information on sales forecasting, inventory, and field sales movement

Selling by means of a norm challenge takes place in a context of three types of values:

1. Each customer's current norms, which reflect the value that one of his critical success functions or businesses is currently contributing to his profits
2. A customer's industry norms, which reflect the average current profit values that all of an industry's similar functions and businesses are currently contributing
3. Your own norms, which reflect optimal values that are competitively more advantageous than either the customer's own norms or his industry's norms

If your own norms represent superior values, you can brand your price at a premium in keeping with your premium value. However, if you can only add enough value to bring a customer closer to his industry's norms, you will be selling a commodity. Industry norms are parity values. They provide no competitively advantageous differentiation. They represent competitive floors, not ceilings. While they may be an improvement over a customer's current norms, the only customers who will aspire to them and be satisfied with them are the permanent and semipermanent residents of their industry's second tier. If you choose them as your partners— or if you are forced to choose them because your norms certify you as a second-tier adder of values—you will grow only as they grow, which will be slowly or not at all.

Industry norms represent standard costs and revenue-to-investment values. They are a compost heap, summarizing the values that many different suppliers' solutions, which have been implemented in many different ways, have contributed to many different customers. A customer who moves up to an industry average may be able to achieve competitive equality. He will not become his industry leader because leadership begins where industry norms leave off.

Learning Competitive Values

If you know your values and your competitors do not know theirs, you have a competitive advantage if you sell on the basis of value. If you know your values and you also know your competitors' values, and they do not know either set of values, you have the greatest competitive advantage of all as a value-based seller.

Of course, if the situation is reversed and they know all the values and you know none of them, you will be at the worst competitive disadvantage if they sell against you on the basis of value.

Competitive values are important for you to know. You may have to sell against them to establish your own values as the industry standard. A second reason you should know them is that your customers may learn them from your competitors' proposals and you should always know what your customers know. The third purpose in learning competitive values is that, like your own values, they are the basis for customer satisfaction or dissatisfaction. The degree of closeness to which they conform to customer "must lists" of required values determines which of you is the most satisfactory supplier.

Whenever you assess your values, you should assess the muchness, soonness, and sureness of the competitive values that may also be contributing simultaneously to your customers' profits. This will require you to measure the same attributes of value that you assess about your own contributions:

- What is the customer's total realized value from each competitor in terms of increased revenues and decreased costs?
- When is payback achieved from the customer's competitive investments?
- What is the customer's rate of return on his competitive investments?
- What are the normative values that customers are receiving from competitive solutions and how satisfied are they with these values?

The implicit question you will want to add to each assay is, How do competitive values compare with our own?

You will need to compare competitive values being contributed to each customer for each critical success function and each critical success business you affect with your own values. Within them, you will need to assess the values that your competitors contribute to each individual critical success factor in each function and line of business. Then you can put together a checklist like this:

- Minimum values on each customer's "must list" that form the hurdle rates for his satisfaction
- Your values and how they compare
- Competitive values and how they compare with your values and with the customer's minimum values on his "must list"

For each category on the checklist, you will need to assess the three specifications of value: how much, how soon, and how sure. Each customer's demand for muchness and soonness in the values he requires will be unique to his own business situation, the life cycle stages of his critical success businesses, and their competitive positions. For every customer, however, the demand for sureness will be universal.

How do your competitors compare with you in the muchness and soonness of their value delivery? If they provide more value, do you provide your value sooner? If they provide more value and sooner, are you the surer supplier? In the final analysis, sureness is the great equalizer. It will always win over all other considerations. Whether or not you can be the highest-value supplier, you must always be the most reliable supplier. Certainty of value, not magnitude, is the keystone to customer satisfaction.

3

Price Your Value

Once you know your value, you can compete on it. This means you must price it. Putting a price on your value is the single most important decision in managing your business because it determines how much you will get back for the value you give; it predicts the return you will be able to command for the investment you have made in the assets that form the capability base of your business.

If you do not base your price on your value, you will end up basing it on your cost or on a competitor's cost if it is lower. In either case, you will be underpricing. You will be giving away your value. Yet this is the only thing you have to sell.

When you base price on cost, plus a "fair profit," you are choosing the lower of two basing points as your pricing platform. It stands to reason that your value must be greater than your cost to produce or supply it. Otherwise you could not remain in business. The difference between the worth of your value and the price you sell it for represents your opportunity loss. The greater it is, the more value that remains unremitted every time you sell.

Businesses that do not know their value routinely underprice. They sell below their worth. They forget that there are two parts to the equation for making money in business. One is to supply value. The other is to get paid for it. Sales must be the function by which you get paid for your value.

Otherwise sales will become the function by which you discount your value and give a part of it away. The cost of your
sales then becomes aggravated by the margins you lose in
discounting your price. This is the double-bogey of competing on the basis of price and performance instead of value.

Subvalue pricing is a fee that is levied on ignorance.
Either you are unaware of your value and cannot adequately
price it or you are aware of your value and cannot adequately
sell it. Managers who cannot sell the value that they know
they have are repressed philanthropists. Managers who do
not know their value are the Rip Van Winkles of business.
They are sleeping through their careers.

Value-based pricing makes a statement that your products and services have their foundation in customer values
and that their prices are an attempt to reflect these values
and realize a commensurate return on the investment to
develop, engineer, manufacture, and market them. This
gives you a method to drive your pricing from your markets.
If your price becomes "too high," your attention will be
called at once to the fact that your value has become too low,
or your market perceives that it has, to support your price.
If your price is too low, however, you will never know it if
you cannot relate it to your value. Too low in relation to
what? you will ask. Because it will probably be comparable to
competitive prices, your price will appear perfectly proper
and the money you are leaving on the table will stay there
until a competitor picks it up or a customer invests it elsewhere.

Avoiding Being Ground Down on Price

From a customer's point of view, value is the sole justification
for price. You must make this your point of view as well.
Nothing else but the contribution of value you make to each
customer's competitive advantage—not your products, your
services, or your systems—can help you avoid being ground
down on price.

Margin control is the essence of management. If your managers cannot manage your margins, they will be unable to assure the source of your wealth. Unless your managers are committed to maximizing margins, you will be willfully stunting your growth. If you think about it, you will realize that your managers are the only force you have available to you for margin defense. Your competitors exist to minimize them. Your customers will do the same unless you help them maximize their own margins first or minimize their equivalent in costs.

Branding is the name of the process by which a product's value comes to justify its premium price. A brand is price-insensitive or, in other words, discount-resistant. This makes it the opposite of a commodity whose value has been discounted by parity competition and whose price is vulnerable to grinding down. Most commodities are ground-down brands. A large proportion of them have lost their brandhood because their original margins based on a unique value were mismanaged.

What does it mean to mismanage a margin? It means associating the margin with its product or service rather than relating it to the values that the product or service can add to customers. The highest risk to margin control is to tie a margin to technology, to today's version of the latest bells and whistles that will quickly be neutralized by competition. As soon as performance becomes homogenized, price follows it to the lowest common denominator.

In order to sustain margin control, you will have to attach your value to the improvement of your customers' critical functions and lines of business instead of to the improvement of your own products or processes. Your value can then appreciate as your customers enhance their competitive advantages rather than depreciate as your competitors destroy your product or process differentiation. *The secret of margin control is to brand your customers with competitive advantage in their own industries and markets.*

By enabling your customers to become branded, you can say to them: "We can help you achieve margin control in your markets by reducing some of your costs that could otherwise prevent you from being a low-cost supplier, and by increasing the values you can add to your own customers that will justify maximum margins. By doing these two things of value for you, we can help you avoid being ground down on price."

This is the apex of partnering, when you and your customers are both branded, so that you receive branded prices from them in return for the value of enabling them to command branded prices from the customers they serve. Only if you brand your customers can you have enough in common with them to partner at a level of mutual maximum margin. This is the best guarantee of shared prosperity for your partnerships. Each partner acts, in effect, as a guarantor of value for the other.

Ruling out Debate on the Merits

Price must always be based on some sort of value. If it cannot be based on the financial values that you add to customer profits, it will be based on the worth of performance values that you add to customer operations. This is "price-performance country," where selling becomes a continuing debate between suppliers and their customers on the relative merits of competitive product performance.

Competitive product evaluation has historically been based on the *how-much question*: How much performance can I, the customer, get for how little price? In many industries, as performance benefits have increased geometrically while their price has fallen arithmetically, the answer has become quite a lot. Customers have been intrigued to find out exactly how little price they need to pay. As a result, they have encouraged and often managed debates whose winners have run up their cost of sales by arguing over more and more finite distinctions that have less and less differentiation. At the same time, their margins hae been run down by the eventual need to sell "at all cost" at any price.

Debate on relative merits inevitably becomes debate on comparative price simply because price comparisons can yield sustainable differences when performance comparisons cannot. In few fields is there a single best product. If there is today, it will not be tomorrow. Only one type of superiority will be demonstrable; a supplier's ability to contribute to customer competitive advantage.

This ability will not be derived from product performance superiorities. First and foremost it will be derived from knowing more than your competitors do about how to bring customer operations closer to a leadership position in cost-effectiveness. Wherever product parity is the rule, the price-performance merits of most products play only a minor role in making customers more competitive. Knowledge of customer operations and markets makes the principal contribution because it allows products to be applied most cost-effectively.

The key to ruling out debate on the merits depends on how you define your "product" because it is to this definition that you will have to attach your price. If you define your product in terms of hardware or software or even service, you will become a debater. Your product's price will be based on its performance. If its performance is perceived to be equal to that of your competitors, the market will act as an equal-opportunity devaluer. No one will make much money.

If, however, you define your product according to its value, you can calculate its worth by the costs it subtracts from customer operations or the revenues and earnings it can add to them. At once you free yourself from debate on performance merits. You free yourself from competitive comparisons of product features and benefits. You free yourself from discounting your price as long as you can substantiate your value in either one or both of two ways:

1. Your cost is less than $1 for each $1 of cost you can reduce or eliminate in a customer's critical success function
2. Your cost is less than $1 for each $1 of revenues or earnings you can increase in a customer's critical success business

Playing the Price Competitor's Game

There are three tiers on which competition can take place:

Tier 1:	Value to value
Tier 2:	Value to price
Tier 3:	Price to price

If you know your value and if you can price it and sell it, you can compete on tiers 1 and 2. You can be competitive with other value-based sellers and with price sellers, allowing you to go head-to-head with value competitors and to dominate sellers who try to compete against your value on the basis of price. On the other hand, if you do not know your value, you will be compelled to compete on price by going head-to-head with other price competitors. Your principal arena of competition will be tier 3, where your products will be marketed as commodities and your customers will be purchasing managers and other cost-controlling functionaries who buy primarily on the basis of price.

Tier 3 is the commodity level of competitive selling. When value sellers try to compete against a price competitor by lowering their own price, they default on their value. There is no way they can lower their price "just a little bit" or lower it "just this once" and then raise it again. Once they play the price competitor's game, they will never be able to sell again on the basis of value. Even if they "win" a sale on price, they lose their margins.

In the mid-1980s, Motorola owned the mobile telephone market. Then, according to Motorola, "the Japanese came into the market and undercut our price by 20 percent with what they claimed to be similar quality. The market bought the quality claim and almost overnight we lost a third of our market share, so we met them head-on. As soon as we went down 20 percent, they went to 30. When we matched them, they went to 35. When we matched them again, they quit. We won. We beat them at their own game."

In reality, it is more likely that the Japanese won. They destabilized the mobile telephone market's perception of value, taking advantage of the fact that neither the incumbent value-based supplier nor his customers knew his value. Lacking hard numbers to prove value, Motorola had no defense. By trading margins for market share, Motorola ended up with less of both in a market that confirmed its suspicions that no significant value differentiation existed. The Japanese, not Motorola, now hold in their hands the advantage of choosing their own time and place for the next round of destabilization. Not only has market control been lost. So has Motorola's control over its business.

Pricing a Customer's Realized Value

Price is either a cost or, if it can be proved to yield a positive return, an investment. Even if it is an investment, until it is paid back it represents an outflow of a customer's current net worth. Once it is paid back and earnings on the investment continue to accrue beyond payback, the resulting profits represent a positive value as the supplier's ability to add to his customer's net worth flows back in. This is what makes a "good deal."

When price is regarded as an investment, its main relevance is the effect it has on payback. The higher the investment, the longer its payback will usually take. This postpones the moment in time when the customer's cash flow on his investment becomes positive, or, to say the same thing in another way, it prolongs the time during which the customer's investment remains at risk. When value is exchanged through investment and return, the deterrence of the "muchness" of a price can be diminished by the "soonness" of its payback.

At payback the customer's original net worth is restored and he is ready, as well as encouraged, to enter the next cycle of value exchange. This explains why it is easier for him to tolerate a higher investment rather than a longer payback. Investment and Return is the name of his game, and without at least the return of his original investments he will not be able to afford to go on playing it for long.

The concept of buying and selling as a *value exchange* also explains why your values, and not your products or services themselves, are your true deliverables. Each sales cycle that you and a customer engage in exchanges a future value that you can deliver for a portion of a customer's present value. Your price tells a customer at once how much of his present value will have to be expended in order to obtain it.

If you do not know your value, you cannot price it and will therefore give it away because the only other basis for price will be your cost. Your customers will also suffer opportunity cost. Being ignorant of the value they can expect in return for each investment with you, they will be unable to plan how and when to optimize its reinvestment. They may miss out on prime opportunities in either of two ways: Opportunities that they did not know they could plan for may come and go or, if the value they realize from you is less than they have budgeted for, they may miss out on opportunities that they have planned because they will be unable to capitalize on them.

Realized value is the only value that counts. It is what a customer can take to the bank because it represent the actual value he achieves. When a customer compares his actual value to his planned value, he can come up with a realization rate on the business he does with you. This is the keystone to his satisfaction with you as a value-adder. As a result, measuring the realization rate of your actual value against your planned value with each major customer must become the cornerstone of your customer satisfaction program. It is the only measurement that will tell you how much you are really adding to your customers' competitive advantage; in turn, this is the only benefit that will ever satisfy them.

Calculating the Base of Value

Instead of trying to improve customer competitiveness by enabling customers to control their acquisition costs by "buying low," value-based pricing improves customer profits by maximizing the return on customer investments. In order to prove this to your customers, you will have to know the comparative values of reducing a customer cost at your full margins versus discounting your product's price. This will enable you to play off cost reduction versus discounting in this way:

> If we give you a 10 percent discount on our product's price, it will translate into a 2 percent reduction in your manufacturing costs, which is where our product will be applied. What if we can give you an 8 percent reduction in your production costs? How much more would that contribute to your competitive advantage as a low-cost supplier? We can do this by reducing your labor content by 10 percent. The only other way to give you the same reduction in manufacturing costs would be for you to find someone to sell to you at a 40 percent discount and, of course, possess an applications and training expertise equivalent to our own.

The fairness of each customer investment, the value-based equivalent of a fair price, is measurable only in proportion to its return. Competitive prices are no guideline. Only competitive rates of return for similar investments under similar conditions of risk are comparable. A "good deal" on a value-based price therefore means three things:

1. The rate of a customer's return on an investment equals or exceeds his minimum hurdle rate.
2. The investment's payback period falls within the customer's patience period for money at risk.
3. The return's value makes a significant addition to customer competitiveness.

Customers calculate the value they can add to their business according to three principles:

1. *Turnover principle*. Turnover is the rate of circulation of the funds that are invested in a business as they start out as cash, become inventories and then receivables, and are finally converted back to cash. Each cycle is one "turn."
2. *Contribution margin principle*. Contribution margin is

the revenue over and above variable costs that contributes to profits.

3. *Return on investment principle.* Return on investment
(ROI) is the ratio of profit compared to the invested
funds required to earn it.

Turnover Principle

If you add value to your customers by increasing their
revenues, you depend on the turnover principle. Turnover
starts with customer cash. Funds flow from cash into inventory when a customer buys from you. Because inventories
are valued at cost and receivables are valued at selling price,
customers put pressure on their sales function to move
inventories so that their invested funds can grow. The difference between receivables and inventories is gross profit. Once
you sell to a customer, you must help him increase his sales
so that he can grow the funds he has invested with you.
Otherwise they will remain "tied up" in inventory.

When funds flow from receivables to cash, they complete
a single turn, as shown in Figure 3-1. During the cycle, the
value of the funds in circulation is reduced by the costs of
selling and administrative expenses. If you can help a customer decrease his sales costs, you can help him preserve his
gross profits.

Gross profits minus sales and operating expenses yield
operating profits. The more gross profits a customer starts
with and the less expense he has to pay out along the way,
the more operating profits he will have left over as the
"return" on his investment with you.

Contribution Margin Principle

Every customer product produces a positive or negative
margin that it contributes to absorbing its fixed costs. Contribution margin is calculated by subtracting a product's variable costs from its sales. In order to increase a product's
contribution margin, you must either help increase its sales
or reduce its variable costs.

When sales are less than fixed costs, contribution margin

Figure 3-1. Turnover cycle.

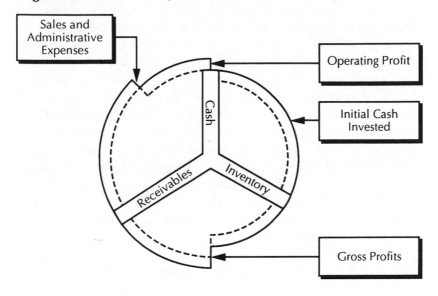

is negative. When contribution margin equals fixed costs, a product breaks even. Above break-even, profits result. New products that have not yet reached break-even, and old, mature products that have accumulated burdensome fixed cost bases are prime candidates for having their contributions improved.

Return on Investment Principle

The rate of return on an investment a customer makes with you is calculated by dividing the resulting operating profit by the total funds invested to achieve it. You can improve ROI by either reducing a customer's total asset costs or increasing his sales, as the formula shows:

$$\frac{\text{Net Operating Profit}}{\text{Sales}} \times \frac{\text{Sales}}{\text{Total Funds Invested}}$$

Calculating Cost and Benefit Values

The rate of customer return, the return's payback period, and the net value of the return's cash flows can all be summarized in a "spec sheet" for value-based selling called a cost-benefit analysis. A model analysis form is shown in Figure 3-2. It calculates the specific financial benefits—the "cash flows"—that can accrue from a customer's investment with you, how long it will take for the cash flows to pay back the investment and what their cumulative amount will most likely be over and above payback, and how the return will flow on a year-by-year basis throughout the useful life of the investment. In Figure 3-2, line 15 shows the net value of an investment's cash flows expressed in terms of present dollars. This will be the customer's *net present value* from the investment. As such it will be the base for your value-based price.

If a price based on your value is going to be a percentage of the net value of a customer's cash flows over the commercial life cycle of his investment to obtain them, what is a fair price for you to ask for the flows of cash? Three ground rules will help you formulate an answer:

1. Price should be calculated so that its contribution to the customer's *actual rate of return,* shown on line 16 of Figure 3-2, helps your proposal equal or exceed his hurdle rate for return on similar investments. This will reassure him that the price he is paying is within his comfort zone for buying capital.
2. Price should be calculated so that its contribution to the customer's *comparative rate of return* helps your proposal equal or exceed the returns from other competitive proposals he may have before him that require similar amounts of investments at similar levels of risk over a similar period of time.
3. Price should be calculated so that its contribution to *payback,* shown on line 12 of Figure 3-2, helps the customer to recover his investment within his patience period so that he can control his exposure to risk. It should also allow him to benefit as early as possible from his investment by receiving positive cash flows, shown on line 11 of the figure, to reinvest in your next proposal. In this way, your successive proposals can become self-capitalizing over time.

Figure 3-2. Cost-benefit analysis.

	Year 0	Year 1[1]	Year 2
1. New equipment investment			
2. Revenue			
3. Cash savings [2]			
4. Noncash expense			
5. Depreciation ACRS [3]			
6. Material trade-in			
7. Profit improvement BIT (3-5+6)			
8. LESS: Income tax (%)			
9. Investment tax credit (10%)			
10. NET PROFIT IMPROVEMENT (7-8+9)			

11. CASH FLOW (1+5+10)			
12. PAYBACK (Cumulative cash flow)			
13. Present value (10% factor)			
14. Discounted cash flow (11×13)			
15. Net present value cash flow (14)			
16. RETURN ON INVESTMENT (10 ÷1)			

[1] Years are annualized, beginning sixty days after installation date.
[2] Cost inflation not accounted for in cash savings.
[3] Depreciation based on 1985 ACRS rates.

A "fair price" is an investment that rewards both you and your customers. It makes a customer's return possible, enabling it to accrue under favorable terms and conditions. It makes your own return profitable as well and provides the funds for your customers to make follow-on reinvestments of portions of each return, which leads to an infinite series of future investments and returns.

Analyzing the costs and benefits of a customer investment, which means comparing the one with the other, reveals what customers get back, their value, from the investments they have to put up to get it. Cost becomes redefined as money that customers must temporarily put at risk in order to make more money. A lower cost of investment may or may not permit a higher return. A high return, on the other hand, will justify a high investment.

Because customers know that it takes money to make money, they understand that value comes first: *How much added value* do we need in order to achieve, maintain, or enhance our competitive advantage as our industry's low-cost manufacturer or market leader? Once that question has been answered, cost can be brought in: *How little added investment* do we need to achieve the added value? The added investment may not be small. But it will always be the least amount of funds that a cost-benefit analysis suggests can achieve the planned added value.

Trading Off Acquisition and Ownership Values

As soon as you divorce your price from the costs of providing the performance values it represents, you will be able to stop customers from evaluating you by their cost control system called "purchasing." Your price will henceforth reflect values that are not product values but financial values that you can add to customer business operations. The evaluation of price can then shift to refer to its values rather than their costs.

When you base your prices on value, you make a statement about them that says your prices can be connected to your customer's profits in two ways. You can reduce some of your customer's costs in excess of your price, thereby improving his profits. Or you can increase some of his revenues and earnings in a similar manner. Either way, you will be able to enter your customer's business management systems where your price will be evaluated as an investment from which a return must be maximized rather than as a cost that must be minimized.

Pricing under a value-based regime permits premium prices as long as you can deliver premium value. Margin control returns to your hands, dependent on the extent to which you are able to improve customer profits. If you can improve them greatly, you can greatly improve your price on a cause-and-effect basis: Your improvement of customer profits will become the cause of your premium price, which will be the effect.

Once your competitors and customers can no longer control your price, you will be freed from dependence on "fair market value." Your customers can use price to reward you for growing their businesses. A discounted price will no longer be the penalty you must pay for your lack of knowledge of how, or by how much, you improve their profits. Price will be what it should be, your reward. It will be the investment you receive for the enhanced return you deliver.

Customer managers who run business units and operating functions above the purchasing level are comfortable with "buying money." They are familiar with the cost of capital. They know the prime rates for borrowed funds. They understand the tradeoff between a return that adds money and the investment required to achieve it.

When they buy your money, customers can put it to work at once. They can invest it in growing their competitive advantage, adding to their assets or paying off their liabilities. When they buy your products, though, they must first convert each product's performance values into cash values. To do this, they must commit direct costs of their own. These dilute the eventual cash value of doing business with you. Customers must also incur the time costs of waiting for the conversion of performance values to cash values to take place. These costs further subtract from the eventual reward.

Finally, your customers may be inefficient in making the conversions of your product values into cash. They may lose value along the way, forfeiting even more from their ultimate profits. It is easy to see why they will be willing to pay you more if you can reduce their direct cost commitments, condense the time before their new profit values flow to them, and prevent lost values by counseling with them on optimizing their application and implementation. In one way or another, they are already paying these costs. Paying a portion of them to you is good value for both of you.

Reducing customer costs immediately improves profits. Shortening the waiting time for profits also improves them. Increasing the operating productivity of customer business functions further increases profits. These are the "ownership benefits" your prices should represent because they are the values your customers will pay a premium to obtain.

The ability to price at a premium is conferred by your markets. You can, and must, plan for it. Your markets, however, make the final disposition. Their decision will be based on two considerations:

1. Do you offer a lower life-cycle cost of ownership as a tradeoff against a higher acquisition cost?
2. Do you offer higher life-cycle sales revenues as a tradeoff against a higher acquisition cost?

For your customers, enjoying low costs of ownership over your product's useful life cycle enables them to justify a high first cost. Based on the total value of their eventual payback, they have the rationale for immediate purchase.

Measuring Your Worth as an Investment

A value-based price has five characteristics:

1. Price is premium price.
2. Price is compared with the improved profits it con-

tributes to a customer's business, not to competitive prices.

3. Price is recoverable by the customer's improved profits and is therefore an investment rather than a cost.
4. Price is not discountable.
5. Price is applications-specific. It varies in direct proportion to each customer's improved profits.

No two contributions to customer profits are ever the same. Therefore no two prices can be the same either.

Price is never the cause of value. Once it is value-based, it becomes the result. Commodity selling makes price the cause. It positions a low price as creating customer value by lowering acquisition cost. Brand pricing turns it around. The customer's value is the financial value added by the brander. This allows price to be positioned as a result of increasing the customer's incremental worth.

By knowing how much value you stand for, you can measure your worth as an investment. You will know how good an option you are as a repository for your customers' discretionary funds. The higher your customer's rate of return and the sooner it accrues, the better an investment you will be. This is the "product" you will install in your customers' businesses, what you will put to work for your customers, and what will improve their profits. When it is a quality product—when its dollar-for-dollar performance is high—you can sell it with confidence, pride, and at a full margin.

The value-basing of price forces you to know the value on which your price will be based. Where can you look to find the value? It will always be in the life style or work style of your customers. Only your customers can make value. It comes out of the way they apply your products and services in their operations, their functions, and their processes. Value is value in use, not measurable at the point of manufacture or the point of sale but only at the point of its application and implementation.

In order to appreciate the fact that value is value in use, suppose that you are a manufacturer and marketer of retail management control systems. This is a mature business with exposed margins. One of your major lines of business is an automated cash management system for gasoline retail chains. It serves major oil company retail outlets and service stations, independent oil service stations, and convenience stores that market gasoline.

These are old, established markets with small margins and burdensome costs. Your systems consist of gas dispenser pumps, electronic control consoles that operate and monitor the pumps, automatic cash registers, automatic service equipment, and data storage and handling capability. Do you sell the systems or their value? Which will help you maximize customer profits? Your own profits?

To the individual gas station retailer, the benefits of your systems are evidenced by more timely profit reports on sales, the flexibility to upgrade his pricing quickly to correspond to peak hours, accurate cost control, inventory control, and reduced labor. Your systems can also lower the costs of customers' station design by saving space and yet still increase the throughput of customer traffic. The retailer's home office benefits as well. It can receive store-by-store sales and inventory data faster and more accurately. The data can be used to reduce costs and improved sales revenues by optimizing delivery schedules to each station. In addition, a supervisor at the head office can manage twelve stations instead of six, saving significant professional labor costs.

In spite of all these apparent advantages, if you sell the management systems by pricing them instead of their value, you will end up discounting them. Because your markets are mature, you will incur high sales costs. You will be positioned by customer cost-control managers as a cost to be reduced. They will ask your sales force for your "best price." If you decide to sell value, you will have to train your sales force to answer questions of another sort:

1. How can profits be maximized at the station level: by solving a customer's inventory problem? By solving a credit problem? Are receipts and distribution out of line? Or is the problem one of labor skills, quality of

maintenance, or the efficiency of present station design and the resulting customer throughput?

2. Is it more profitable to reconstruct a customer's stations to increase traffic or is it more cost-effective to improve the customer's profit contribution from the existing layout?

3. How can profits be improved at the customer's home office level: Is there a data control and reporting problem or a problem with cash management or the speed or quality of decisions made by supervisory management?

4. What are the total costs to be reduced? What are the total sales revenues to be gained? What are the customer's investment offsets required to achieve these results? What improved net profit is most likely to result to the customer? By when? What is the return on his investment?

Instead of asking your sales force, "What is your 'best price'?" their customers will ask, "What is our best inventory per station? How much should improved stock control contribute to station profits? Is stock control more valuable to us than cash control or credit control right now? What is an acceptable penalty to pay for a slight excess inventory to ensure against being out of stock at peak driving times?" For each solution to such value-based customer problems, you have the ability to command a value-based price.

Equating Investment With Short-Term Loans

Customers are no exceptions to the rule that investors want prompt payback and maximum returns, a common fantasy known as eating their cake and having it too. For many customers, investments of the type you will be proposing when you sell value will be funded from current cash flows because the investments are incremental to a customer's annual budget; that is, they are opportunistic and their return is not calculated as a percentage of the customer's total asset base. This gives them a comparatively high yield, often in three figures representing a rate of return of hundreds of percentage points. Depending on how much of the investment must be front-end loaded, payback can often be achieved well within a project's first year. This is especially true of revenue-expansion projects or projects that can combine new revenue streams with cost reduction.

When payback can be this quickly achieved by a customer and carries with it a high degree of sureness, an incremental investment becomes the equivalent of a short-term loan in return for a high rate of interest.

Lending money to you is a whole lot more palatable to customers than spending money with you, especially at profitable rates of interest that exceed the hurdle rate of a customer's cost of capital when he becomes a borrower of funds. A loan whose principal is sure to come back fast and fattened is an attractive investment. Both the principal and interest can be put back to work at once to earn more money. If you have a compelling follow-on proposal, they can be put back to work with you. In this way, your customers can keep recycling the interest on their original loans in short-term successive increments to fund one profit-improvement project after another.

At the point where the cumulative interest that a customer has received on a series of paid-back "loans" has become significant, he comes into a unique position. By reinvesting the interest he has earned on his loans to you, he is playing with "found money," new funds that are neither a part of his capital resources nor earned from continuing operations but money you have helped him obtain: It is therefore "our money," mutually earned by and for the partnership of the two of you. By all rights, the partnership should have first call on the recycling of the returns from investments as long as it can propose fast, reliable returns at competitive rates.

The loan-theory of incremental investments is useful in proving three characteristics of what constitutes a customer's concept of a "good price": quick turnover, an acceptable profit each time it turns, and a safe bet to turn quickly and profitably. These are the best prices to pay because they come back to the payer. The only cost he has to guard against is the opportunity cost of missing a competitive investment for the same funds whose price would be returned even more quickly or at a more acceptable rate of return. But the nature of funds is that they must always be at work. If you can offer steady short-term employment for customer funds, you will have a competitive advantage over sporadic, periodic opportunities and proposals with longer paybacks that offer less secure moneymakers.

Pricing at a Floating Point

As your value varies from customer to customer and from one critical function or business line to another even within the same customer's business, prices that are based on your value will vary with it. There will be no such thing as "list price"; indeed, there will be no price list at all for value-based sales and therefore nothing from which to discount. The concept of "price" for all but frank commodities will disappear. A product with a price will be declaring itself to be a commodity.

Value-based selling is selling whose value is based on results. As results change, the price of value will change accordingly. This means that price becomes a floating point that is always being driven by value and that automatically renegotiates itself around the value that drives it.

The computerization of a fast-food business offers an example of floating-point pricing. If McDonald's invests several million dollars with IBM to automate its inventories of hamburgers and fries so they will never be out of stock, what is the value of its investment: the cost of computer hardware and software? The value will be found in the profits from the incremental sales that its stores are able to make as a result of always having sufficient stock on hand. If IBM and McDonald's agree on what that number should be, it can become the point around which IBM will set its price based on the added value to McDonald's of its added sales. This price will then become a floating point.

As long as McDonald's incremental sales targets are achieved, IBM will receive its price. If McDonald's loses sales revenues because it is out of stock, the negative value of these lost sales can be deducted from the price. IBM's price will then fall back to an ongoing base fee in payment for its managerial performance. Conversely, as McDonald's business grows, so will IBM's price.

IBM has already adapted a performance-based pricing strategy to sell personal computers to elementary school systems. When IBM installs its equipment, it trains a school's teachers and counsels with them on how to improve their students' reading scores. If the scores improve up to or beyond a guaranteed norm, IBM receives a guaranteed fee. Otherwise, IBM will be paid only a cost-based fee for its up-front work. IBM's hardware and software carry no price. The sole basis for IBM's price is the added value it can contribute to a school system's objectives in improving its "customers' " competitiveness.

A guarantee is actually a way of tying compensation to performance—a form of incentive-based compensation for the guarantor. In advertising, a minimum guarantee of the sales performance of an advertiser's products, not the readership or viewership performance of its agency's advertising, could become the basis for agency compensation. DDB Needham Worldwide has begun to guarantee the sales results of its advertising in this manner. In return, it asks for a 33 percent bonus on its base commission rates if the agreed-on sales objectives are met. Two thirds of the bonus goes directly to the agency people who create the advertising. If objectives like increased market share are not met within a specific time frame, the agency will rebate up to 30 percent of the commission payment.

In order to control the variables that can affect advertising's impact on sales, DDB Needham acts as a systems integrator of a client's total marketing communications mix that includes direct mail, sales promotion, and public relations.

Floating point approaches to pricing protect a customer

against downside risk and, at the same time, reward the supplier for upside gains over and above a customer's most likely objectives. Value-based prices, whether in the form of a one-time payment or recurrent fees, royalties, or bonuses, have to put a floor under the customer but should put no ceiling on the supplier's compensation for upside gain. This positions *price as the result of value,* which is exactly what it should be in every customer-driven relationship.

Guaranteeing Value to Eliminate Price Consideration

Incurring a cost, even when it is an investment, is always something of a risk. Money is out and although it is being managed and therefore is presumed to be under control, no control is foolproof. The unexpected is a constant threat. All or some of an investment may be lost. Additional funds may have to be invested to rescue it. Or it may be fully recovered later than needed, postponing payback and causing a customer to have to borrow capital to make up for its shortfall or forego other investments whose timing has been predicated on the return of the original funds.

Customers and their suppliers have learned several methods for reducing risk that have become integral parts of all investment proposals. They make conservative estimates of return. They know that it almost always takes longer than it seems to reach payback, so they stretch out their breakeven points. They set frequent milestones to measure the flow of funds so they can make sure that they are on schedule or they can take prompt remedial action if they are not. They form joint ventures to sponsor major investments in order to share the risk. But 101 ways of reducing risk are not equal to one way to eliminate it as a consideration.

Value that can be guaranteed is the one and only way to remove the price of an investment as a reason not to go ahead. Other reasons may keep an investment from being a good deal: Its return may be too small or its payback may be too late, for example. But price will no longer be a factor because it will be divorced from the risk of failing to achieve the proposed value it is being allocated to earn.

Guaranteeing your value does not mean making a meaningless promise such as "100 percent satisfaction" or a mealy-mouthed pledge of "your money back" such as "If you have a problem, we will fix it to your satisfaction at no added charge or adjust the bill—or you do not have to pay."

Returning a customer's investment after he has not made his return does not make him whole again. In the meantime, while his money has been out, he has been deprived of any other use of it. He has therefore incurred opportunity loss, which is the incremental value of other potential returns he could have earned if he had invested the money elsewhere or with someone else. Nor does "your money back" take into consideration other direct and indirect costs a customer may have expended to support his investment with you. For these reasons, guaranteeing value must mean "your return back."

A guarantee of value introduces certainty into the eternal question, Should we invest? It substitutes "Why not?" for "Why?" One way or the other, a customer can be sure of receiving value that is as much as he bargained for at the time when he bargained for it. It is the ultimate no-risk proposition.

Once the certainty of return has been made implicit, the major constraint against investing in value falls away. Very few customers can afford to ignore a sure thing. You will have to determine whether you can afford to offer it. If you know the normal values you deliver—your "norms"—you will always be safe staying to the left-hand side of the mid-range of your values. This way, you will err on the side of conservatism. There are three considerations that should enter into your guarantees:

1. A conservative estimate of the value of the total cumulative net profits that you will most likely be able to deliver to each customer from each proposal and its corresponding rate of return. This means less, not more.

2. A conservative estimate of the amount of time you will most likely require. This means more, not less.
3. A conservative estimate of when the customer will most likely achieve payback. This means later, not sooner.

In order to be able to deliver on your guarantees, you must always stay within the experience of your norms and make sure that each proposal you guarantee is for "a normal project"; that is, the same kind of project from which your *norms* have been derived, where all the critical success factors are similar and no single critical success factor is outside your normal experience.

Opening a Customer to Value-Based Pricing

Value-based suppliers position themselves by their openers. Their first words define their expertise and thereby their pricing policy by telling what they are good at doing and with whom they are good at doing it. In this way, they position the nature and the amounts of their value and the way they intend to be compensated for it.

If you base your business on value, you will eschew "vendorese," the language of vendors. In one way or another, through semantic subterfuge and linguistic legerdemain, vendorese speaks to customers in variations of its basic theme of "Have I got a *product* for you." Sometimes vendors substitute the word *system* for product. At other times, they use the word *solution*. In any event, it is immediately clear that products are being sold, and that they are going to be priced on their comparative performance features and benefits.

Based on what your customers' businesses are all about, profits, you must be a reducer of the customer's costs that you can affect and an increaser of customer productivity and profitable sales volume. Your openers will come easily in this context:

I know the critical success functions on which you rely.
I know where the critical cost factors cluster in each

> function. I know what they now average in other businesses similar to your own where I have reduced them. Compare your costs to my norms. If your costs are higher I can help you bring them down. If they are already low, I can help you keep them low or make them even lower.
>
> I hold the standard norms for productivity in critical success functions like yours. If your productivity is below my norms, I can help you improve your output per worker by reducing downtime, reducing scrap, and reducing defects that can lead to product recall. If your productivity is above my norms, I can help you keep it that way or make it even better.

Tyro suppliers will pause here and ask their customers to take a function, any function, where an improved contribution to profits would be meaningful. Professional suppliers will come prepared with their own proposals. They will have already scoped their customer's business. They will know where they can begin. They will know by approximately how much they can help. They will know how soon their help can start to flow. They will know the customer investment required to fund it—the customer's price. They will enter by offering the *value of the new dollars they can add to a customer's business*. This value will be the end point of their calculations. But it will be the starting point of their customer partnerships.

Adopting the Xomox Model

Xomox Corporation is a manufacturer of sleeve valves. Since Xomox valves have the same basic form and function as valves that were found in the ruins of Pompeii from A.D. 79, it is an understatement to say that Xomox is a mature industry. Not only that, it is oversupplied by dozens of manufacturers. Yet Xomox, a small company, has consistently earned a 30 percent average return on equity as the reward for its value.

The Xomox strategy of competing on the basis of value is threefold: concentrate, customize, and consult.

Xomox *concentrates* on a single product line of valves that it sells principally to the petrochemicals industry. It knows its customers' industry.

Xomox *customizes* its valves to fit a small number of its customers' critical success functions. It knows its customers' processes.

Xomox *consults* on the applications engineering of its valves and bases its prices, which are always set at a premium, on the value it adds to each customer's functions by decreasing their costs or improving the productivity of their throughput. It is paid for the values it adds, not for the valves it sells. The value is an amalgam of several component parts, the most important of which are applications services and customer training. But the core value is Xomox's knowledge of its customers' critical processing functions. It knows where the costs cluster, by how much it can reduce them, and what the dollar value of these reduced costs normally amounts to. It also knows where productivity can be improved the most, by how much output can be predictably expanded, and what the added dollar value normally amounts to from the increased output.

Xomox knows more about how to add value to customer processes to reduce their costs and increase their productivity than either its customers or competitors know. That is one part of its value-based positioning. The other part is that Xomox knows more about how to apply its products and services to generate predictable profits for its customers than either its customers can achieve alone or its competitors can achieve for them.

Xomox enjoys its premier position because it is an *applier of chemicals processing technology* instead of merely a *supplier of process valves*. What Xomox actually applies, however, is maximum added value to critical customer success functions.

When Xomox sells its customized profit-improvement solutions, it does not enter a customer's business bearing product "spec sheets," catalogs or brochures, or even the products themselves. They stay in the car. Xomox presents its two partnering tools. One is its norms, supported by case history testimonials that prove its track record of value. The second is a proposal to improve the customer's profits according to its track record's norms.

Realizing the Competitive Advantages of Branding

When you base your business on adding value to your customers, you "brand" it. Branding is the strategy of customer advantaging. By enriching your customers, you add to their competitiveness. In the process, you brand your business as competitively advantaged as well. You become a grower, a conferrer of improved profits on your markets. Profits are your products. You sell money. Instead of asking, "What can we sell this customer?" you ask, "How can we add competitive value to his business?"

Until you can answer this question, you have no customer for your value because you have no product—nothing to sell until you find a value you can add and nothing to price because the value will determine your price. Just as your values will always be customer specific, so will your prices.

The customer-specific nature of value attests that your value differentiates each of your customers when it is added to their businesses. If you sell like a vendor, pricing your performance based on standard product features and benefits, you lose this ability to offer differentiation. Every customer is sold the same product. As a brander, you can make your distinctiveness pivotal to your profits. Instead of sharing the vendor's obsession with making his competitors into losers, you can become obsessed with making your customers into winners.

If you add only product values and stop there, you will be fighting burnt-out wars. You will be the Continental Can Company competing with its econoweld™ seamless can against the American Can Company and its miraseam™ seamless can. Customers will run their fingers nimbly over your comparative seams and, finding parity, compel a differentiation between you by running roughshod over your price lists.

If you add your values solely to your products and not to your customers, you will run the risk of being the Lincoln of the 1960s through the 1980s to your industry's version of Cadillac. For most of those three decades, Cadillac regularly outsold Lincoln by margins of up to 6 to 1 although Lincoln was, many of these years, a technically superior automobile. Cadillac's added customer value showed up at trade-in, which certified its cars' superior return on investment. Cadillac made Lincoln noncompetitive, every year superseding Lincoln's current performance values by its own assured financial values.

Without effective rebuttal, Cadillac was able to deposition Lincoln as a debatable option by saying about itself, "Cadillac is one of the few material possessions for which there is no true substitute." Once competitors can no longer be regarded as true substitutes, you have ended the possibility of debate on comparable merits and can obtain for yourself a transient monopoly, the blue ribbon prize for valuing your value.

4

Sell Your Value

When you sell "normally," that is, based on the values you can normally add to your customers' businesses, you can condense your traditional sales cycle by one- to two-thirds. You can say that normally you are able to help your professional service customers increase their revenue per engagement by 25 percent, for example, or normally you can decrease downtime for manufacturers of consumer appliances by 5 percent within ninety days; or increase the order-fill rates of petrochemical processors by 33 percent in three months.

If any of your norms is superior to a customer's current values, you will have found a *quantified* prospect. You will have uncovered a need in the form of a value deficit. This is not the same as a need for a computer, for example, or the need for a risk management system or for telemarketing. It is a need to rejuvenate a value, to repair and replenish it so that it no longer shows the deficit that is creating a competitive disadvantage for your customer.

Your norms for adding value should be your competitive stock-in-trade. No matter what you make, you will be able to sell from your norms. Otherwise, your customers will be unable to forecast the added value that you represent. They will only be able to forecast your contribution to their added costs. Because costs are negative values, customers will require you to minimize them at the outset by discounting your prices and to justify the remainder.

Figure 4-1 shows the value hierarchy pyramid. At each level, value has its own meaning:

- If you vend at the purchasing management level, "value" will be interpreted as the lowest price for the highest performance benefits.
- If you sell to higher-level management, "value" to a middle manager is a profitable solution to a cost problem or a revenue-generating opportunity. At the top level, the solution is less interesting than the profits it can add and the improved productivity of corporate assets that it will permit. At these levels, product features and their performance benefits are meaningless;

Figure 4-1. The value hierarchy.

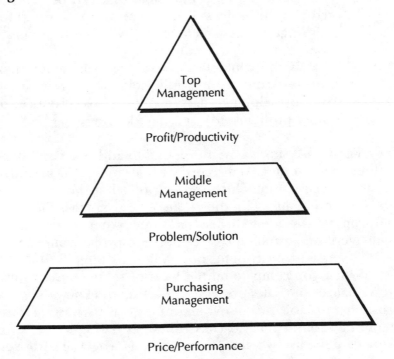

they have no value. Price that cannot be translated into an investment and correlated with its normal return is equally irrelevant.

A value-based sales proposal made to the middle and top levels of the customer pyramid follows an outline like this:

1. Here are our norms for the maximum cost values that our experience says this business function should be contributing to your total costs—or for the minimum dollar values that this type of business line should be contributing to your total revenues. How do your costs and revenues compare with our norms? If your costs exceed them, you are incurring an unnecessary expense. If your revenues lag behind our norms, you are incurring an unnecessary opportunity cost.
2. What is the added profit value that can be contributed by your business function or line of business for each single percentage point by which you can more closely approach our norms?
3. What is the competitive advantage this amount of improved contribution will yield to your business, either by helping to make it a lower-cost producer or a more profitable market share leader?

Figure 4-2 shows how a proposal to add to a customer's value can be summarized according to its most critical contributions, each one of which can be proved at the same time to be in conformity with the range of your norms. This type of proposal is made to order for "value owners," the middle managers of customer cost centers or profit centers who always need to contribute more value to their businesses.

When you compete on the basis of value, you can professionalize your sales process. You will always know the right customer to call on. You can dispense with wasting time scouting around for "coaches" to act as dating services for you or debating whether a customer is a technical buyer,

Figure 4-2. Proposed added values vs. norms.

	Proposed Added Value ($000)	Norm ($000)
1. Cost Savings	$ 450	$ 350–$ 650
2. Revenue Expansion	950	800– 1,000
3. Total Added Value	$1,400	$1,350–$1,650
4. Current Sales (%)	0.8	0.6–0.8
5. Payback (Months)	4.1	4.0–6.3

economic buyer, or strategic buyer. If he or she is a current value owner, you have the right customer.

You can tuck your so-called high-gain questions in your back pocket and devote yourself to presenting "high-gain answers" to customers needing to become competitively advantaged. Instead of positioning yourself as a supplicant by asking to receive value, you can give it. You can let your competitors walk around with their blank needs-benefits analysis questionnaires that delay the sales cycle's getting to proposal. You, meanwhile, can go directly to a value owner with a cost-benefit analysis of added value.

Searching and Valuing as the Way to Sell

By directing your customers' attention to their own operations, processes, and functions, you will focus them on their management mission and make them aware of the opportunity you represent to help them perform it better. Most of them need to improve their use of available technology to increase sales, to expand output by speeding up production, to reduce wasted time in product design and lost time in manufacturing, and to make more competitively marketable products instead of scrap. If you can help them to achieve such improvements whose value exceeds their cost, you will be able to give them a competitive advantage.

As an illustration, if you are expert in improving the value that can be contributed by your customers' manufacturing functions, how should you sell your expertise?

Suppose you add value to the manufacturing functions of automobile makers. The critical success factor you concentrate on is work station productivity. By redesigning the 20 percent of all the stations on an assembly line that contribute up to 80 percent of its productivity, you can normally increase by 30 to 40 percent the amount of time in which each worker is actually adding value to every car rather than standing by idly or walking around picking up parts. As a result of your work, the plants you redesign normally require only 3.36 workers for each car per day compared with their competitors who normally require 4.38 to 4.99 workers. This gives your customers a significant competitive advantage as low-cost manufacturers.

Suppose that the industry norm for changeover time to comprehensively redesign an automobile chassis is approximately seven to nine years. Suppose your customers are normally accomplishing it within four years. A single selling sentence asking, "What would the value be to you for each one year we can help you come closer to our norm?" can establish your competitive value.

When you sell from value-added norms, the technological wizardry that supports the values remains in the background. Suppose you decide that the best way you can add maximum value to a customer's manufacturing process is to replace some of his people with precision machines whose quality never varies. Accordingly, your technology will be based on arrays of robots connected to lasers that will check their work. Does your customer have a passion for robots and lasers? Or does he have a passion for the values they can add to his cars so that "people in the front and back seats can talk to each other at 60 miles an hour?" Based on your answer, what should you be selling?

Suppose your customer's principal competitor has decided that keeping people involved in the production process is the only way to assure craftsmanship. Now how should you sell? Should you specify the leading-edge advantages of your technology against the state of the art of your own competitors or should you calculate the optimal mix of human labor and robotics and move your customer one percent at a time toward these values? In this way, the customer's certainty of maintaining control over his operations can be preserved from the threats of automating too much or too soon.

"What are you measured by?" you should get used to asking your customer managers. "Is it the annual percentage rate of your business growth? Managers in your industry with whom we work normally average an annual gain of 5 percent. Is it your trial-to-repurchase ratio? Our norm is a 55 to 65 percent conversion of tryers. Is it the percent of orders filled on time? Our norm is 99 percent. Is it receivables collection? Our norm is within 30 days. Is it inventory turns? Our annual norm is 6 to 8. Is it the ratio of revenue to investment? Our norm is 30 to 35 to 1."

Prospective customers will identify themselves by their deviations from your norms. Your search-and-value teams—men and women you used to think of as "sales representatives"—can deploy across your major industries searching for them, holding your norms like templates before them. The templates will represent your rated capacities to improve customer profits. Your capacities will be rated by your experience, not in making products that work better but in making your customer work groups better workers. To detect deviations that they can improve, your search-and-value teams will place their templates one by one over each customer's critical success factors and say something like this: "Here is an expense that falls significantly outside the boundary of our norms. It is making an unacceptable cost contribution. What would the added value be to you if it is brought one percent closer to our norms?" "Here," they will say, "are revenues that fall significantly inside the boundary of our norms for this product category. What would the added value be to you if they are brought one percent closer to our norms?"

Positioning as a Valuebringer

Ever since they became required writing if not required
reading, mission statements that attempt to position a company with its markets have frequently been emission statements. They have been flatulent with corporate piety and
self-proclaimed virtues. Almost every mission statement sets
forth the exclamation points of what a company makes and
sells instead of the values they bring to their customers. They
enshrine the company's own products and processes in pref-
erence to their contributions to the products and processes
of its markets. Ask yourself: "Does your mission statement
position you as a valuebringer? Does it dedicate you to
adding value to the customers you serve? Does it define the
values you add to them?"

If you are a supplier of health care systems, do you
declare your mission to be reducing your hospital customers'
costs of providing quality care or increasing your home
health care customers' sources and amounts of revenues? If
you are a supplier of computer systems, do you declare your
mission to be reducing your manufacturing customers' costs
of product design or increasing the revenues of your customers who manage lines of business by "helping them make
more and better decisions faster"? If you are a supplier of
telecommunications systems, do you declare your mission to
be reducing your customers' costs of collecting their receivables or increasing their revenues by providing real-time
stocking and inventory reports?

As a valuebringer, your experience is your most valuable
possession. It says that you know how you can apply your
expertise to a customer's business. It also says that you know
how the customer functions and business lines you sell into
generate their costs and revenues; where their most cost-
intensive problems and revenue-intensive opportunities can
be found and how long it normally takes, how much it
normally costs, and how much value you can normally add
by making your impact on them.

To be experienced as a valuebringer means that you

have done it successfully before, permitting a customer to infer that you can do it again. Your norms will speak for your accomplishments. You can present them as an average value or a range. If you present them as a range of values, you will be able to say that you have never added less value than the low end of your range and have never added more than your high-end number. Using these norms as a template, you can compare a customer's current performance standards to your experience standard. If he falls outside the acceptable boundaries of your normative impact on costs, you can bring him closer inside. If he falls inside the boundaries of your acceptable normative impact on revenues, you can bring him closer to the outside of your range.

Norms are never generalizable. They are function specific on the cost side and business specific on the revenue side. Certainty resides in respecting the specificity of your norms. Trouble comes from trying to generalize from them. If you propose outside the range of your norms, you are throwing away your experience. You and a customer will be going where neither of you has ever been before.

Each customer whose profits you improve becomes the next contributor to your norms. A poor job will lower your norms. A superior performance adds to their high end, perhaps even extending it to an all-time high. The safe way is to use the range of your norms as book ends and to try to bisect their median point in each proposal. The leadership way is to keep pushing out against the high end. A value-based sales scenario has four steps:

1. *The norm challenge.* By confronting a customer with your norms, you encourage him to test his current performance against your standards.
2. *Norm envy.* After comparing, the customer discovers one or more of your norms to be superior, arousing "norm envy" for the opportunity to increase his competitive advantage.
3. *Deprivation anxiety.* With his need aroused, the customer calculates the added value of approaching your norm and determines it to be significant.

4. *Request for proposal.* Fortified by his calculations, the customer asks for a specific quotation of how much added value you can propose, how soon it will accrue to him, what his investment will have to be to obtain it, and what rate of return it will most likely yield.

Selling From a 3 × 5 Card

Your norms are your trump card in selling value. If you put them on a card, you can deal them to your customers from the top of the deck as the best way of developing leads.

Figure 4-3 shows a 3 × 5 norm card used to sell automated process control systems to pulp and paper plant managers. These value owners are at the top of the customer hierarchy in Figure 4-1. The norm card lists the critical success factors that account for up to 80 percent of a plant manager's costs. For each critical cost factor, the norm card specifies the supplier's average contribution to savings in dollars per ton for a typical 250,000 tons-per-year mill.

The critical success factors listed on the norm card are the value levers of the plant manager's business. Not only do

Figure 4-3. 3 × 5 norm card.

Critical Success Factors	Total Savings ($/Ton)
Salaries, Wages, Benefits	$ 4.0
Chemicals	4.6
Wood	2.3
Energy	2.1
Total	$13.0
For a typical 250,000 TPY mill	$3.25 M

they manipulate value more than any other factors; they also have a multiplier effect on value because, in the mature pulp and paper industry, even minor changes in their contributions to profits can generate major changes in a supplier's competitive advantage.

The process control system's sales force deals the norm card on its first calls and issues this kind of norm challenge:

> In which of these factors that are critical to making your mill a lower-cost competitor can our normal savings give you the most immediate advantage? Let us begin to work with you there at once and then progressively expand the initial advantage one by one to each of the other critical factors. The savings you generate from each cost reduction will fund the next successive project.

The 3 × 5 card in Figure 4-3 shows how a picture can be worth a thousand words. Other norm cards can say at a glance all of the following:

> For an industrial manufacturer of your size and product mix, we are normally able to contribute an average value of $1.6 million in year 1 to the reduction of your inventory management costs. This value comes from improving the accuracy of your forecasting capability, which we have found to be the critical success factor that will enable you to fill enough additional orders the same day they are received to realize the added value we are proposing.
>
> For a supermarket chain of your volume and store distribution, we are normally able to contribute an average value of $3.2 million within the first eighteen months to the revenues generated by your major stores' dry cereals sections. This value comes from more profitably allocating your product mix between high-margin and high-turnover brands and maintaining full stocking of these major moneymakers at all times. We have found these to be the critical success factors that will enable you to make enough additional profitable sales to realize the added value we are proposing.

Differentiating Within Customer Standards

In many industries, customers are imposing "open standards" on their suppliers that mandate common performance criteria to which all suppliers must conform. By enforcing commonality, customers are legislating the commoditization of their suppliers' businesses. With the possibility of putting a value on proprietary features and benefits ruled out, meaningful performance differentiation has all but been eliminated as a basis for price.

Suppliers are being standardized because their customers are finding that the costs of integrating and interconnecting incompatible equipment and retraining their people to operate it can nullify the advantages of proprietary values. We want our new equipment to be plug-compatible with our current base, they say. We want to train our people once and have them be able to operate any equipment anywhere in our organization the minute they sit down in front of it. As open standards proliferate and as universal parity replaces proprietary performance uniqueness, how can value differentiation be preserved? How can you prevent the margin erosion that accompanies a customer-legislated utility type of business?

Once product-driven values have been homogenized and proposals based on proprietary standards are declared ineligible to compete, advantages derived from traditional concepts of value are instantly neutralized. No one can be better than anyone else. If added value can no longer be attributed to anybody's product, a price tag can no longer be affixed to it. Otherwise it will only reflect commodity values. Where can price be attached?

Customers in open standard markets are saying to their suppliers that their own competitive differentiation does not come from the suppliers' systems they own but from the ways in which they are integrated and implemented. Applications functions must become the new value-adders. How good are you at managing the integration of your systems with multivendor systems so that they maximize the total contribution to customer profits? How good are you at training customer operating people to maximize a total system's cost-effectiveness?

Open standards dictate a revolutionary value shift. It is no longer the performance values you put into a product that will predict its price. It is the project management and work-group training skills you possess that provide the value base for price. Product R&D, engineering, manufacturing, and quality control all take place on your premises. Management of customer operations and training customer people take place on your customer's premises. As soon as the basis for value creation is relocated from manufacture to end use, the place where it occurs changes from your control to customer control.

You must learn how to apply your value to each customer's critical success business operations and critical success function processes. That is where his systems contribute significantly to unnecessary costs or fail to contribute necessary revenues. It is where his people are unnecessarily underproductive or manage their operations in an unnecessarily cost-ineffective manner.

If you have become comfortable adding value on your own shop floors or in your own office environments, you will have to undergo a culture change that enables you to perform value-adding in customer offices and plants. You will be working with customer people, not just your own. You will be working on polyglot customer systems, not just your own. You will be engaged in protracted beta tests that, unlike the old-fashioned experimental kind, will be real. They will determine your value.

When you are within a customer's grasp, you will have no recourse against being customer driven. His norms, which will be made obvious to you, will be your base of operations. Your values, which are the improvements you make in your customer's norms, will also be readily apparent to you. You will be seeing the actual incrementation of your value as your customers have always seen it, *in use*.

Proposing Something of Value

If you sell only values you can measure, you will always be selling from your strength. You will be able to stay comfortably within the arena of your experience where your track record proves you can be reliable as a value-adder. This should help you to maximize your sales. At the same time, by measuring the values you sell, you will always know where you stand in customer satisfaction.

Once you commit to selling your measured values, you can lay your norm templates over a customer's current performance, calculate the improvements you can make, and propose to add your values everywhere they apply:

> For your manufacturing managers, what if we can add the value of a minimum 25 percent reduction in scrap costs, allowing them to become competitively advantaged over the industry's current lowest-cost producer?
>
> For your sales managers, what if we can add the value of allowing each of their sales representatives to spend 15 percent more time with their customers, increasing the number of major customers called on two or more times each month by an average of 30 percent?
>
> For your plant managers, what if we can add the value of reducing the average length of downtime by 5 percent while also increasing meantime between downtimes by 15 percent? What if we can increase the number of orders they can fill the same day they are received by 60 percent?
>
> For your chief financial officer, what if we can add value to his collection function by reducing outstanding receivables by an average of twelve days?
>
> For your brand managers, what if we can add a minimum of 5 percent to their realized volume objectives? At the same time, what if we can also add a minimum of 3 percent to their share goals? What if we can add a minimum of 36 percent to their brands' repurchase-to-trial rate? What if we can add a minimum of 150 percent to the average payout of their brand's promotion programs?

While you are proposing the value of buying your added contributions to profit, each customer manager will be putting a value on buying your added costs.

In order to put a value on "buying costs," a customer will apply payback analysis to see how fast his costs can be recovered by your cost savings or your help in increasing his sales. He will also discount the resulting future cash flows so that he can determine their present value in today's dollars. Finally, he will compare the added cost savings or added income to his investment with you to determine its rate of return.

When a manager at any level of a customer's hierarchy incurs new costs as a result of doing business with you, he knows that his only chance of ever seeing value will be through the depreciation allowances he can get on his taxes and the savings or increased sales he can get from the operations you affect. He can be sure of the depreciation; the rest is conjecture. He also knows that whatever values he receives will be further reduced by the costs of depreciation as well as the continuing costs of maintaining and upgrading what he buys.

From a customer manager's point of view, the purchase of incremental costs entails three categories of expenditure. First there are *costs of acquisition* such as requesting and evaluating quotes; placing purchase orders; and inspecting, certifying, and processing deliveries. Then there are the *costs of possession* that are incurred when inventories are created. These include rent, taxes, labor, insurance, interest paid on borrowed funds, damage, deterioration and obsolescence costs, and opportunity costs resulting from capital tied up in inventory that might have been invested more profitably elsewhere. Finally, there are *costs of ownership* that are the sum total of all the operating costs incurred over the investment's commercial life. All of these expenditures represent negative values. In order to make a sale, your positive values will have to counteract them.

Adding Value Throughout the Life Cycle

If you position your business as an adder of values that can reduce your customers' costs, you will get the attention of two kinds of customers:

1. Start-up businesses that want to avoid unnecessary sunk costs
2. Mature businesses that want to reduce unnecessary operating costs

If you position your business as an adder of values that can expand your customers' revenues, you will get the attention of two kinds of customers:

1. Start-up businesses that want to grow fast
2. Growth businesses that want to keep growing fast

If you can add value in both ways, by cost reduction as well as revenue expansion, you can be a full partner to any customer. Otherwise, you can only be a half partner. Whichever half you choose presents a paradox. It is easier to prove your value from cost reduction because direct costs are hard numbers. Revenue expansion, on the other hand, represents a correction of opportunity losses whose numbers are softer and more subject to assumption. But no customer can save his way to prosperity. Sooner or later, he must increase earnings and revenues if he is going to grow. Revenue expansion, which is more difficult than cost reduction to quantify as well as to achieve, is more necessary if you are going to play a compelling role as a value-adding business partner.

If you can expand significant new revenues for your customers, they can tolerate unnecessary costs. But if you can only reduce costs, they cannot long tolerate the lack of new revenues without falling into the most stagnant mode of business, stability.

A stable business is going nowhere, neither growing nor declining. It is indecisive, inactive, and indolent. Decisions take forever, postponed by the hope that the need for them will go away while they are being deliberated. A stable business lives in constant fear. Its managers are afraid to attempt to grow the business because, if they fail, the burden of an added investment without a commensurate return may plunge the business into decline. As a result, managers of stable businesses characteristically look down, not up, awaiting the fall and suspecting that every action—indeed, any action—will destablize the tentative balance between their earnings and expenses.

Stable businesses are candidates for the values of cost reduction but only if the costs to be reduced significantly exceed the costs incurred to reduce them and if results are sure to show up quickly. To help make certain that this will always be the case, stable business managers invest as little as possible. When they do, they invest against the chance, however slight, that the funds may prove unrecoverable. Even if their investments are productive, their returns on this tentative, toe-in-the-water basis are likely to be equally small. The consequent net improvement in the value of their businesses is apt to be miniscule.

Businesses in stability may be growable but their managers generally do not dare to grow them. The managers have simply lost their dynamic. Only when their businesses start to decline can you get their attention, for then there will be no choice. The fear of falling, which induces paralysis during stability, is gone. The fear of going belly-up, which induces action, replaces it.

Proposing to Add Value to Customers in Start-Up

Start-ups can be your future major customers. At start-up, however, businesses represent major risks both to you and to themselves. Start-up is the single most crucial phase of the business life cycle. Entry and growth, the two following phases, are preconditioned by start-up. A good start will not necessarily predict good growth. But a poor start will foredoom it.

If a value-addable customer is a new start-up venture within a mature corporation, the manager's prime objective is to progress quickly through his start-up cycle to move out of "the garage" and into his market as soon as possible. He is living on a borrowed budget on borrowed time. His top-level management will wait only so long for him to produce results. His competitors will not wait at all. Meanwhile, for every day that passes, his market opportunity window will be closing.

What strategy should you take? Because you know that market entry is a start-up manager's fixation, your proposals to add value should focus on it. Can you help the manager make his entry on time? Even better, earlier? Less expensively? Can you help him stay in the market once he gets there by ensuring his product's reliability and avoiding recall? Can you help him make sure he is choosing the right market and positioning himself properly as its premier value-adder?

A proposal to add value to a start-up can be based on cost avoidance before market entry or it can be based on preventing opportunity loss of sales after entry.

Before market entry, a new business is a collection of sunk costs. While its asset base is being laid down, nothing is available for sale. Hence, its cash flow is completely negative. Its capital funds are being invested at a high rate of expenditure. Everything is going out and going out fast and nothing is coming in.

How many of these costs can you help avoid? Every dollar saved at start-up has the value of a dollar-plus earned later. A dollar that can be saved can immediately be invested elsewhere. Or it can be returned to the start-up's sponsor, which lowers its total investment and, by reducing its eventual breakeven point, speeds payback.

Start-ups are heavily into cost displacement or cost replacement. Your proposals should therefore try to wipe out a cost category or consolidate several costs into a single lower cost. They should substitute a less costly solution for a more costly one.

The second way to add to start-up value is by reducing opportunity costs that can delay market entry or can come back to haunt a business as "would haves-could haves-should haves" after it has been commercialized. These opportunity areas typically involve four business functions: market analysis to make sure the market is rightly assessed from the start; product and process design to make sure that the product is right for the market and is manufactured cost-effectively; quality assurance to make sure that the product will not incur excessive warranty costs for repair, replacement, or recall; and forecasting and inventory control to make sure that the product is neither backordered, causing lost sales, nor overstocked, causing excessive handling, storage, and insurance costs.

Proposing to Add Value to Customers in Entry

Entry is the make-or-break event for a business. It furnishes the proof of start-up. The test of a successful start-up is how little needs to be done at entry, or redone, to refine and redefine the start-up's strategies. At entry, a good start-up should need only to standardize volume operations.

Entry provides the first checkpoint at which market segmentation can be evaluated. Has the right market been selected? Entry also validates the business's value-to-price ratio. Will the market pay full margins for its value? The growth phase yet to come depends on the accuracy of these start-up decisions. If they are wrong at entry, growth will be delayed or denied. The business may have to go back to the drawing board—that is, back to start-up—for rework or it may be deep-sixed for good.

Helping a start-up business make entry on time and on plan, and then pass through entry as quickly as possible to begin growth, is the greatest contribution to its value you can make. Only by reaching breakeven does a business become a commercial entity. Up to then it is merely an investment, an act of faith that there may be a business opportunity. The onset of positive cash flow confers validation.

If a value-addable customer is just entering a market, the manager's prime objective is to consolidate his toehold into a firm foothold by achieving first positive cash flow. Every unnecessary day below breakeven adds to his costs, postpones his profits, and increases his vulnerability to competitive knock-off. His top management's patience time may run out or a competitor may become preemptively positioned first. The market's money may, as a result, go elsewhere.

What strategy should you take? Because you know that breakeven and its onset of positive cash flow are an entrant manager's fixations, your proposals to add value should focus on them. Can you help the manager enter his market faster? Less expensively? Can you help him maintain his product within specifications and in stock? Can you help him bill and collect receivables faster to ensure his cash flow? Can you help him remain differentiated from predatory competitors who are attracted by his success yet unencumbered by his sunk costs?

A proposal to add value to an entry business can be based on revenue expansion or it can be based on preventing the opportunity loss of sales.

Immediately on market entry, a business presses for breakeven. This is the milestone that signals the payback of its founding investment. To achieve continuing growth, it must focus on expanding revenues and earnings from sales. How can more incremental revenue dollars be brought in? How much faster can they be booked? How much faster can they be collected and converted into receipts? Or, to say the same things in other words, how fast can the market be penetrated, how fully and completely can its opportunity be capitalized, and how great a share of market can be realized?

Proposing to Add Value to Customers in Growth

The growth phase of a business is its finest hour. Everything that has been planned for so long can finally come together in the race for market share. Time is of the essence. Demand, once provoked, must be fulfilled. Competition, once enticed, must be preempted.

Two other events mark growth. Product quality set at entry must be maintained so that reliability becomes commonplace. Reliability with no surprises is the keystone to growth. Its assurance must be warranted. Demand, growing apace, must be fully met. Every unmet unit of demand represents unrecoverable opportunity loss.

A proposal to add value to a growth business must address three areas of customer need: You must help maximize volume, help control standardization, and help generate follow-on products that will become members of a growth family.

If a value-addable customer is growing, the manager's prime objective is to continue to grow at a steady or increasing rate. If his rate of growth slows, maturity may overtake the business and the opportunity to become a big winner will be lost. If the market for the business is growing and the customer is growing below par with it, then each dollar of unmade sales growth represents opportunity loss that can never be made up.

What strategy should you take? Because you know that the growth rate is a growth manager's fixation, your proposals to add value should focus on it. Can you help the manager ensure his productivity, minimize downtime, and assure reliability by manufacturing a standard product with near-zero defects? Can you help increase sales to the original market and extend them into adjacent markets? Can you help control variable costs that invariably inflate with volume? Can you help prepare for the first product proliferation that will extend the initial line into a product family?

A proposal to add value to a growth business must be based on supporting or accelerating the customer's rate of growth.

A customer's growth phase has two objectives. The first is to maximize his market share by selling up to the full manufacturing capacity of the business. This gives a growth business its insatiable appetite for cash. Its cash flow must therefore be assured. It is a sin to lose sales because of lack of cash or capacity. Nothing suffocates growth like the inability to get product out the door except the inability to keep it from coming back. How much faster can the customer's business be grown? How much faster can his inventory be turned and his receivables collected? How can downtime be minimized and quality maintained?

A customer's second objective in the growth phase is to prepare the business for its next entry. A successful market entry not only justifies proliferation; it demands it if lost opportunity is to be avoided. Market acceptance offers opportunity for market expansion. How cost-effectively can a second entry follow? What economies can be gained by sharing asset bases? How can the initial product's reputation for quality be bred into the next product? How can tie-in sales create a system for selling the first and second products together?

The transcendent purpose of growth is to perpetuate growth. How long can a growth rate of sales and profit making be maintained? Because growth is a rate and not a state, every additional day that the rate of growth can be sustained is an added day of premium profits, one day more during which the onset of the declining margins of maturity can be postponed.

Proposing to Add Value to Customers in Maturity

A customer in maturity has an upside and a downside. By the time a business becomes mature, its managers know just about everything that has to do with how it should be run. This is its upside. This is also its downside. Knowing everything—what works and what does not—it is difficult to innovate. Lack of innovation is precisely why a business becomes mature in the first place.

At maturity, the volume dependency that has been built up in growth becomes chronic. The learning curve that brings down unit costs in inverse proportion to volume is a stern taskmaster. As volume becomes relentless, the pressure mounts to increase the share of market necessary to absorb it. This can usually be accomplished only by accepting progressively higher sales costs and lower margins. As a result, costs become a mature customer's main preoccupation.

If a value-addable customer is mature, the manager's prime objective is to ensure the competitiveness of his business by reducing its costs and increasing its productivity. In a mature industry where commodity products have lost their differentiation and where the size of the total market is no longer expandable, low cost and increased cost-effectiveness are the only available contributors to margin protection.

What strategy should you take? Because you know that

cost control and productivity improvement are a mature manager's fixations, your proposals to add value should focus on them. Can you help the manager reduce his labor content? Can you help reduce scrap and downtime? Can you help increase his volume without increasing costs? Can you decrease his sales costs? Can you add product value through progressive marginal renovation? Can you increase market share? Can you preserve his installed customer base against missionary competition?

A proposal to add value to a mature business must be based on delaying the decline of profits or sales that is the inevitable result of the end point of growth. Even though volume at maturity may be huge, decaying margins and rising costs absorb revenues at an increasing rate as maturity progresses. The mature phase of a business requires a delicate balance between maintaining or increasing sales yet maintaining or decreasing costs, including the cost of sales. The expansion of sales comes harder in mature markets where the markets themselves are not growing and increased penetration requires the conquest of a portion of a competitor's share. How can sales be increased cost-effectively? How can current sales be maintained more economically? How can the product be renovated marginally to provide a sales incentive yet keep costs down? How can costs—any costs, all costs—be better controlled?

Mature proposals must focus heavily on productivity improvement as a means of increasing customer output at lower or the same cost. By the time a business becomes mature, its assets have become a mixed blessing. They provide the capability base. But they are also the cost base. Can they be reduced? Can they be modernized? Can they be made more productive by buying instead of making, leasing instead of buying, or operating jointly instead of going it alone?

Just as growth proposals are dedicated to perpetuating the growth phase, mature proposals must perpetuate the business as long as it can go on yielding an acceptable rate of return on its assets before the assets become more valuable than their return.

Understanding the Customer Connection

Every critical success function you touch in a customer's business is connected to another function and every one of its critical success factors is connected to one or more other factors. Customer operations are networks of interconnections. You cannot affect one operation without creating positive or negative ramifications in another. Positive ramifications will enhance your proposed values by adding to them through the sympathetic reaction of one improved function with its correlate functions. This is synergy. Negative ramifications, on the other hand, can deplete or destroy your original values.

Because of the interconnectivity of customer operations, value is affected by multiple factors that you may not be used to taking into consideration and by people, processes, and proclivities that you know little or nothing about. When you propose adding value to a customer, you must be aware of the human and operations networks in his business that will become your total value network. How can you get all the major components of your network, the 20 percent that provides 80 percent of the result, to add value to each other instead of subtract it?

First of all, you must know where each function you are proposing to work on is connected and how its connections both influence it and are influenced by it. Next, you must know the amount of influence that is most likely to be passed along and the time frames in which these transactions customarily take place. In affecting a product's design cycle, for example, how much cost will it add to the customer's investment to ensure quality control and marketability after you speed up the cycle? How much high-priced labor will be involved? Will a new database have to be set up? New software programs written for it? New test and measurement equipment installed or existing systems recalibrated?

In the case of a packaged good's sales cycle, how much cost will the customer add to his investment by upgrading his inventory control system, integrating it with his forecasting system, and networking the two together so that potential regional shortfalls can be detected in advance of promotions?

If you neglect your networking, you will be consigning yourself to the risks of partial realization of your proposed values or to complete failure for reasons you may never know. Networking acknowledges that changing a single factor in a business, however significant it may be, rarely changes the business significantly all by itself. It also pays respect to the dangers of indulging in simplistic *if-then* thinking:

- *If* you increase the time a customer's sales force can stand before its customers, *then* you will automatically increase its sales.
- *If* you convert a customer's inventory to a just-in-time basis, *then* you will automatically decrease its costs.

What is time-before-the-customer connected to: What does it depend on? What costs and commitments are released from a salesperson's schedule to make it available? What are the cost and operating tradeoffs involved? What is the expected hit ratio of sales per the number of added calls made? How can the quality of the new customers being called on be assured so that sales can be made at full margins? These questions involve connected issues that must be taken into account before you can try to arrive at your value.

What is just-in-time inventory connected to: What other functions does it depend on? What is the new role of the forecasting function? How will suppliers be connected to the system and which suppliers will be selected? What is the proper proportion of just-in-case standby inventory to just-in-time delivery? How can freed-up space best be converted to productive uses? These questions involve connected issues that must be taken into account before you can try to arrive at your value.

You can never go wrong by assuming that nothing and no one stands alone in a customer's business. When you introduce one change, no matter how benevolent, you simultaneously alter other operations whose mix of plus and minus contributions to your value must be calculated as part of your proposals. They will give you more to think about as a valuebringer. Consequently, they will also give you more to sell.

5

Control Your Value

Your job in helping customers run their businesses more competitively is to help them control the values they bring to their own customers. You must help them control their quality. You must help them control their cash flows, their order entry and inventory, their productivity, their most crucial costs, and their most crucial revenue generators. If they lose control of their vital functions, they can lose their competitive advantage or their ability to recoup it. If you lose control of your ability to add your value to your customers' vital functions, you will lose your own competitive advantage. This will show up in the damaged profitability of your sales. The self-portrait of your situation will come to resemble the dreaded sales/profit relationship shown in Figure 5-1, where heavily discounted sales beginning in year 4 have increased revenues but made them profitless by year 5.

The ability to control your value—its manufacture, delivery, application and installation, and measurement—is your only basis for marketability at consistent high margins.

Value control requires eternal vigilance. The management of value always threatens to escape control. Zenith says that the quality must go in before the name goes on. But that is only the beginning. Your quality is not your value; it is only a source of potential value. It is not enough for quality to go in. Its full value must come out if it is to yield a benefit. Quality must be applied before that can happen. It must be

Figure 5-1. Sales/profit relationship.

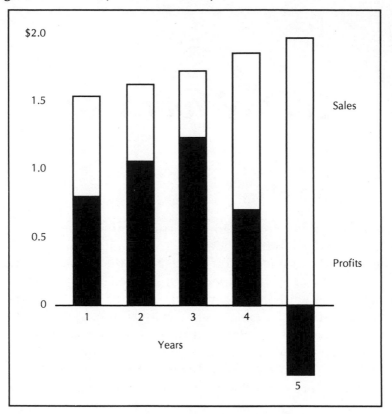

installed in a customer's business and implemented knowl-
edgeably by his people. They must be trained to get it out.
They need information, education, and consultation. Other
suppliers' quality must be integrated with your own. You may
want to partner with them to ensure its value. You may even
want to manage the customer facilities you supply in order
to certify that the application of your quality will be maximized.

Your customers' main hope of controlling their value is
for you and their other major suppliers to control the value
of what you sell to them. Your value is the basis for your
claim to partnership. You must have sufficient value to present yourself as partnerable. Thereafter, you must be able to
control your value so that you can guarantee its reliability in

order to retain your partnership. If certainty passes into suspicion or evidence that your value can vary, that it is no longer predictably "under control," your partnership will be at risk even though your value may be superior to the stable value of a competitor.

Qualifying Quality in Respect to Value

Just as the quality of a product does not equal its value to a customer, superior quality does not automatically convey superior value. The relationship between quality and value is not necessarily one-to-one; sometimes it is inverse if the value that the customer gets out of a product is less than the potential value of the quality that has been built into it. This is more often the case than not. Value is rarely delivered by products alone. A customer must apply it to his operations and implement it into his functions by training his people to maximize your product performance, counseling with them on managing your processes for maximum contribution of profit, and providing an on-line measuring and monitoring system to evaluate your contribution.

The role of product quality in contributing to customer value has three characteristics:

1. Product quality must be good enough to contribute to a customer's satisfaction with your value.
2. Product quality must not make a negative contribution to a customer's satisfaction with your value.
3. If product quality is superior to competition, it must be accompanied by superior applications services to make sure that your quality is fully realized by each customer.

Superior product quality requires an equal need for applications quality if your customers are going to be able to get full value out of their investment to acquire it. The difference between a customer's actual realized value and his full potential value is the opportunity cost of the lost chance to maximize your mutual profits. If you try to use the value that can be contributed by your product quality as a substitute for the value added by applications and implementation, information, education, and customer consultation, you will be driving your business from your laboratory, your plants, and a vendor sales force rather than from your customers. You will be free of the costs of having to understand your customers' businesses, but you will more than pay the penalty with reduced margins.

Before you dedicate yourself to engineering and manufacturing a certain level of product quality, you should have the answers to two questions:

1. How little quality do you have to build into your product to help maximize its contribution to customer satisfaction?
2. How much quality do you have to build into your product-support services to help maximize the customer's total satisfaction with your value?

By asking yourself how little quality you need in your product rather than how much, you will force yourself to build it to customer specifications of "enough value," not your own. This is not a plea for shoddy goods. It is the best way for you to remind yourself that quality that does not contribute to customer satisfaction is waste, an added cost to both of you instead of an added value. It is also the best way to remember that the value that gives your customers their competitive advantage is in the hands of the applier rather than the developer.

Becoming Interested in Reliability

Leading technology is allegedly on the edge of value contribution. By being more productive and cost-effective than lagging edge counterparts, new-wave capabilities are supposed to offer competitive advantages. But very often they do not. Leading edge frequently turns into a bleeding edge.

As a result, many customers agree with Carl Reichardt of Wells Fargo, who has said, "I am much more interested in reliability than being on the leading edge."

In the metaphor of the razor and the blades, the razor represents a customer's major initial investment. It is typically defined as "the product" because it is physically tangible; often it is capital intensive. The consumables that it requires in order to operate, including supplies and support services such as training, maintenance, and repair, are referred to as the blades. The razor is a one-time or long-term purchase. The blades incur repetitive life-cycle costs that add up to the ongoing costs of ownership. When a razor and its blades are bundled into a single packaged sale, a system results.

It has been said that if equipment is the razor and its support services are the blades, the key to customer satisfaction—that is, the key to value—is to "get damn creative on the blades." There is good reason for this. The blades are where the value is. They are also where the cost is. In an automated factory, for example, the highest costs are for applications and training, not for equipment. The rule of thumb says that for every dollar spent on hardware, ten dollars must be spent on software and one hundred dollars on training.

The major problems of the leading edge are generally in the blades, not the razor. The blades must impart three kinds of value:

1. They must be valuable in themselves.
2. They must ensure the full delivery of the razor's value.
3. By their positive values, they must compensate for any negative values contributed by the razor.

There is no longer much differentiated value added by "razors" no matter what type of hardware is involved. There is also a rapidly decreasing value from many traditional services, such as maintenance. The Maytag repairman with nothing to do is a symbol of the increasing reliability of many products. If your products are in this category of reliability, you may be able to add some temporary value by getting into multivendor maintenance of your competitors' products. But sooner rather than later, you will learn that a value-based definition of service must focus on the total facilities management of customer operations. Anything less is a disservice to your own growth and represents a nonservice to your customers.

Blades are a razor's insurance policy, guaranteeing the reliability of its delivery of value. Of all three attributes of value—muchness, soonness, and sureness—the certainty of its realization is paramount. The greatest value ever designed by "the trembling hand of man under the benign gaze of God" is useless if it cannot be depended on. Sporadic, periodic, and nomadic value can be more trouble than it is worth. Businesses are run on predictability, not promise. This is why "better" is so often the enemy of "good enough."

Surprise is the antithesis of predictability. No manager can afford surprise. Even if a result exceeds his expectations, he will not have been able to plan to utilize it fully or on time, and so a significant portion of its full value may be wasted.

Value that comes out of applications comes out of knowledge of customer businesses, not your own. That is why Unisys Healthcare Systems, a supplier of computer hardware and software systems to hospitals, says that it needs "healthcare professionals, not data processing people" who can help Unisys bring "an applications solution focus to what has traditionally been a hardware business."

Solutions are in people's heads, not in computers. Shipping computers to its hospital customers simply transfers costs from Unisys to them. Only when the computer systems can be applied by knowledgeable people to solve customer problems and seize customer opportunities can value be transferred. And only when value flows can both partners make money. Its surge will be wasted, even destructive, if it cannot be controlled. If the surprise is on the downside, expectations will go unfulfilled and plans remain unmet as costs remain unpaid.

Customers must be able to expect the values they will

receive and to receive the values they expect. If you cannot be relied on for the delivery of as much value as you propose within the time you have proposed to deliver it, the highness of your high technology will be nullified by the lowness of your reliability. Lesser performance that is dependable will always be preferred to peaks of superior performance interspersed among valleys of disappointment: A straight line of revenues and earnings, which forms the baseline for planning, is always more manageable than a sawtooth.

When you sell value, reliability must be your middle name. What you propose must be what each customer gets. If you are on the leading edge, your challenge is to convert it into reliable value. This must be largely accomplished by the units of information that accompany your product units in the forms of customer coaching, counseling, and consulting.

Becoming Comfortable With Good Enoughness

Unless you believe in the good-enoughness of quality, you will reflexively return to the drawing board to add quality to your products whenever you need to improve their value-to-price relationship. All you may actually be adding is cost. The "Good Enoughness" curve in Figure 5-2 shows how the Pareto principle applies to product development. The first 20 percent of investment generally yields 80 percent of the benefits. If the "good enough" point can be reached within this range, good enough to contribute the values that will satisfy your customers, you can maximize your value at minimum cost. The more you invest beyond this point, the deeper you will be penetrating into "six sigma country," where the remaining 80 percent of your investment will yield only 20 percent or so of the remaining benefits as the 100.0 level of perfection is approached.

How little of this incremental quality do you require, not how much, to satisfy your customer needs for value? When you go beyond this point, and you must know your customers' values in order to know where it is, your added costs will

Figure 5-2. "Good enoughness" curve.

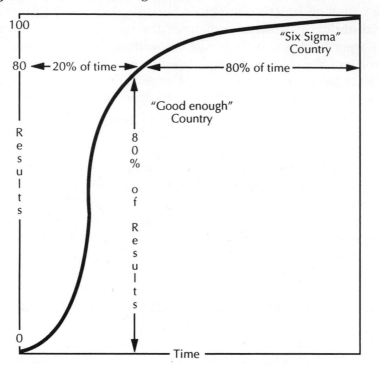

begin to unbalance your value-to-price relationship. As your price rises to recover them, you may find that your excess value is unmarketable; in other words, it will be unaffordable and because it is too much, your price will be regarded as too high.

Not only may your costs be unrecoverable but you may also lose market share because your customers can see no competitive advantage for themselves in subsidizing your excess value.

The strategy of good-enoughness is designed to prevent insufficient value as well as value that is in excess of what a customer needs or is able to implement. Enoughness sets both a minimum and a maximum standard, falling midway between "not enough" and "more than enough." This is the zone you must control in your business so that you can help your customers control their own businesses.

Controlling the "enoughness zone" of product quality is what quality control should be all about. It confirms the customer drive of your business. When you are "in the zone," you are capable of helping your customers the most. You are also capable of helping yourself. The good-enough zone is your signal to get off the S-curve you are working on and redeploy your development assets to start a new curve. Unless you do, you risk throwing bad money after good to make what is already good enough even better. While you continue to tweak quality, you leave your competitors free to launch new S-curves that can obsolete your current values with a new technology or new applications of an existing science.

If this occurs, you will succumb to the "one more generation syndrome" that spells doom to the quality tweakers who seek what they believe to be the remaining marginal increment: companies like Lockheed that tried to coax one more generation out of piston aircraft while Boeing was obsoleting piston technology with jets, like Baldwin that tried to extract one more generation out of steam locomotives while General Electric was obsoleting steam technology with electric engines, and like U.S. Steel that tried to squeeze one more generation out of open-hearth furnaces while international competitors in Germany and Japan were obsoleting open hearths with basic oxygen.

Reality-Testing Your Value Performance

Everyone in your business who is a value-adder, and that should include everyone in your business, must have standards of performance for value creation and delivery. These standards should be driven by customer satisfaction so that they include criteria like these:

- Every appropriations request for funds should be your most cost-effective answer to the question, Is it the minimum investment to maximize customer satisfaction at the customer's good-enough level? If not, it should go back to the drawing board.

- Every proposal to add value to a customer should be the best resolution of muchness and soonness that is consistent with your norms for sureness.
- Every product, service, or system should conform to the following criteria:
  - —Its value cannot be significantly improved without a significant additional investment on your part that would be reflected in customer dissatisfaction with the cost of its acquisition or ownership.
  - —Your investment in it cannot be significantly reduced without a significant reduction in value that would be reflected in reduced customer satisfaction.
  - —Therefore, value can neither be added nor removed without significantly reducing customer satisfaction.

A growth council of customer representatives can offer a forum for a periodic reality testing of your values.

Growth council members ought to be mirror images of your business. If you are an adder of values that help customers reduce or eliminate costs, your council should be composed of value-owners of critical success factors in your customer's cost functions. If your added values help customers improve revenues and earnings, your council should be composed of value owners of critical success factors in your customers' profit-centered businesses. From time to time, you may want to supplement them with support people from their operations, especially technical and financial people.

Your agenda with each growth council meeting will need to address value issues of the what-if variety such as the following:

- What if we could add this much value to this critical success factor, what would the value be to you? How much value would be good enough? What would a fair investment be? What would the hurdle rate for minimum acceptable return on such an investment be? When would payback be required?
- What if such a new value were available now? What kind and amount of interruptions would it impose on

your current operations? What delays in getting back up to speed again do you envision? What retraining of your work groups would be required? Would it all be worthwhile?

- What if you could have a wish list of alternate values instead of the ones we are proposing? What would you add? What would you eliminate? What would you alter? What impacts do you envision these changes would make on your current values or costs of implementing them? How much would they most likely be? What would your level of satisfaction be with them?

A customer growth council can serve two indispensable purposes. For one, its members can be your initial *value testers* at the alpha level and later in on-site form at the beta level. Second, they can act as your *value attesters* after beta testing, providing you with data for your model cost-benefit analyses and testimonial case histories from which to make your first sales.

Basing Standards of Performance on Value

When you compete on value, the standards of your managers' performance should be based on the amount and timeliness of value that each of them contributes to your customers. For some managers, the standard of value performance will be met when customer revenues or earnings are expanded. These managers will be in sales, sales support applications, product development, and brand or product management. For other managers, the standard of value performance will be met when customer costs are avoided or reduced. These managers will tend to be primarily involved with making products and applying them to customer operations.

Every manager whose contribution to customer value can be measured should have it standardized in the form of a minimum acceptable performance. This can broaden the base of your people who are able to position themselves as value-adders, extending whenever appropriate to research and development, engineering, and manufacturing.

When you standardize value performance, you make your business customer-driven at a single stroke. There is no longer any escape from driving your business according to the same standards that your customers apply to you: How much are you adding to their competitive advantage? When all of your critical function and critical business managers are performing according to value objectives, you can incorporate two control mechanisms into the way you operate. You can compensate for value and you can budget on it.

Compensating for Value

When value becomes a performance standard, you can compensate each manager for his and her contribution to customer satisfaction. Either a percentage of salary or a percentage of bonus can be pegged to the achievement of satisfaction values: Was the planned "muchness" delivered to each customer within the planned "soonness" that was committed to in the customer's account plan? The percentages you allocate will indicate how seriously to take value as the basis for your competitiveness. The low end of your reward system should never be below 20 percent. At the high end, 40 to 60 percent says that you put customer satisfaction at the top of your priorities as a business objective. Figure 5-3 shows the contribution to bonus that Chrysler allocates to customer satisfaction.

Figure 5-3. Chrysler bonus formula.

Profits	20%
Market Share	20%
Product Quality	40%
Customer Satisfaction	20%

Every manager who is significantly compensated for contributing customer value has a built-in competitive advantage in partnering with customer correlates. I am paid the same way you are, your managers can say, on the basis of the values I add to your business. I can prosper only insofar as I help you prosper. If you accept me as your partner, you will never have to be concerned about my proposals being self-serving. Unless they serve you too, they will disserve us both.

Budgeting on Value

Your standards of value performance can also be used as the basis for the flow of funds you allocate to your business managers. Funds can flow first to the highest value-adding managers of cost centers or profit-making lines of business. The answer to "How can I get budget?" for every manager of a current operation can be biased by his or her track record as a valuebringer. The motto "Funds flow to value" can symbolize your obsession to grow the businesses and functions that are chiefly responsible for growing your customers, the ones that keep you competitive and grow your own business in return.

Taking the Pledge to Be a Value-Adder

Henry Armstrong, the trumpeter, was talking of musical values when he said, "If you ain't got it in you, you can't blow it out." But having it in you is no guarantee that you will be able to blow it out; that is, that you will be able to apply it to your customers' businesses and business functions so that the value you have put into your products and services comes out as a satisfactory contribution to their competitiveness.

Most businesses are long on putting value in and short on making sure that it comes out. Managers routinely dedicate their businesses to provide popular values but say little or nothing about enforcing their application. The "purpose of Motorola" is typical:

> The purpose of Motorola is to honorably serve the needs
> of the community by providing products and services of
> superior quality at a fair price to our customers.

In keeping with its objective to provide some of its products at the "six sigma" level of quality, leaving little room for imperfections or defects, Motorola also commits to provide service with "uncompromising integrity" by people who are "best in class." As a result, Motorola feels safe in assuming that its customers automatically derive the full values these investments represent so that their operations, not just Motorola products and services, can function at a six sigma level of their own. Motorola makes no commitment to this objective, which is customer-driven and not driven by Motorola manufacturing or engineering. Yet it is the only pledge of value that matters.

A revised pledge based on customer satisfaction rather than self-satisfaction might read like this:

> The purpose of Motorola is to add competitive values to
> the businesses and business functions of our customers
> that will enable them to operate at lower costs and
> higher revenues and earnings so that they will be more
> profitable, thereby being better able to serve their own
> needs and the needs of their communities.

This kind of pledge is dedicated to help customers do their jobs better, that is, to control the values they deliver to their major markets. The pledge captures the difference between a company like Motorola that is trying to control its own operations and a company that is trying to help customers control the critical operations in their own businesses. The first type of commitment is internal, driven by a manufacturing mentality. The second type is customer-driven, external in its focus, and reveals a market-oriented mindset.

Xerox is another manufacturing-minded company that believes "improving total quality management" is the key to value. At Xerox this process is called "leadership through quality" and it is designed to take place by continually striving "to listen to customer requirements and to meet those requirements." Yet when customer requirements are truly listened to, unfiltered by product-related tell and sell, something like the following is usually heard:

> Make me more competitive. Help me maximize my own customers' satisfaction in doing business with me. Let me offer values whose cost-effectiveness in improving my customers' profits will be my industry's standard; no one will be able to be better. This means that my value must be good enough to maximize satisfaction by reducing my customers' costs as much as they can be cost-effectively reduced or by increasing my customers' revenues and earnings as much as they can be cost-effectively increased. I emphasize cost-effectiveness for two reasons: First, I must be able to afford the values you can add to me that will make me more valuable to my customers and they, in turn, must be able to afford to buy my values from me. Second, I must be a reliable supplier of my values. I must be able to control their dependability. This means you must be able to control your own reliability as a value-adder to me.

> These two reasons dictate that your value to me must be good enough. If it is less than that, it will be cost-ineffective. If it is more than that, you will over-engineer it. As a result, you will overcost it. If it is too exotic, you will not be able to maintain its quality control and so my reliability will be at risk. So will my affordability.

Seeking Costs That Can Improve Customer Profits

Cost control typically concerns itself with "unnecessary" costs that can be avoided, reduced, or eliminated altogether. Yet in value-based competition, costs in the form of investments that can add to your value capabilities, which means they pay back a positive net return, should be actively sought. These "necessary costs" will be the foundation of your true competitive asset base because they will give you your unique abilities to improve customer profits.

It can be beneficial for you to set up two classes of costs:

1. *Performing costs* that you can invest in facilities, resources, and capabilities that add enhanced profits to your customers
2. *Nonperforming costs,* a correlate of nonperforming assets, that do not add significant quantifiable value to your customers

In these terms, corporate policy would maximize your investments in performance costs and minimize nonperforming costs. The highest expected customer values from each investment would dictate funding. In this way, your allocation of growth resources will always be in step with your customers' financial targets because you will be adding value to the same critical success factors in their businesses that they are. When you are all budgeting for the same values to accelerate customer competitiveness, you have taken the concept of growth partnering to its ultimate destination, the corporate kitty. It is all well and good to say that partnerships depend on mutual objectives. In the final analysis, their dependence is based on mutual funding.

Where are you putting your money? When you compete on value, it must be put where your customers' mouths are; that is to say, in the same place where they are investing their own funds.

When you budget to invest in performing costs first, you force your managers to build their business cases around customer value. How many dollars must I fund to assure customer competitiveness? How many dollars will my customers fund me back in return? The answers to these two questions should be on page one of every business plan. In capsule form, they describe the essential facts about a business: how good it is at converting your dollars into customer values and how good it is at maximizing the dollars it gets back in return for those values. That is the steak of any business. The rest is parsley.

Performing costs return their investments over varying time frames. Some costs pay back quickly. They bring instant relief to a customer, adding immediately useful values to customer competitiveness. Other costs germinate for a while and take longer for customers to capitalize or for you to pay back and earn your own realization.

Certain values flow in a steady stream once they start. Others are not only delayed but behave erratically once they flow, obeying not so much their manager's objectives as ebbs and flows in short-term business cycles, technology cycles, seasonal cycles, or applications cycles in a customer industry. This may have as much to do with your customers' budgeting processes and their sense of priority about performing costs as with your own. One value may preempt another, interrupting an applications rollout and resulting in an uneven flow of values. At other times, one value may have to supersede another of lesser urgency.

Getting Into the Value Business

When you convert a product-based or service-based business into one that is value-based so that you can enter wholeheartedly into "the value business," you will need to be able to deliver on three things:

1. Your value will have to have *applicability*. It will have to be specifically applicable to the customer needs for added value that you set yourself up to satisfy in terms of its enoughness and soonness. This will enable you to position yourself as a customer specialist.
2. Your value will have to have *reliability*. It will have to be dependably deliverable in terms of its enoughness and soonness so that your customers can plan on it and so that you can guarantee it. This means that your quality control processes and procedures must focus on ensuring your value. This will be the only way that your customers can control their own value's reliability to their own markets.

3. Your value will have to have *affordability*. It will have to be comfortable for customers to invest in because they will receive sufficient enoughness or soonness to achieve payback quickly, encouraging them to set up a perpetual cycle of invest-return-reinvest.

If you can deliver value that your customers can apply to their competitive advantage, that is dependable, and that is affordable because the relations between investment, return, reward, and risk are weighted preponderantly to return and reward, you will be able to maximize your own competitive advantage as a value-adder.

When this happens, you will find that getting into the value business makes three claims on your capabilities. First, you will have to equip yourself with a knowledge of your customers' current values, both positive and negative, so you can know what their costs, revenues, and earnings amount to. Second, you will have to learn your customers' deviations from your normal values so you can know how much more costs and how much less revenues and earnings they have in comparison to your norms. This knowledge will set your targets for adding new values.

Third, you will have to know how much new value you can contribute to reducing customer costs or increasing revenues and earnings by bringing them closer to your norms. This will tell you how much you can help customers become lower-cost suppliers or market leaders.

Giving Customers a Controlling Interest

Because your margins are at the mercy of your values, your single most crucial mission must be to control your values. You must keep quality high; you must keep reliability dependable and predictable; and you must control consistency so that you never run out of premium values to sell nor let your competitors preempt the state of the art of your values. Once you surrender value leadership, that is, you are no longer the most reliable contributor to maximum competitive advantage for your customers, you may never regain it. Even if you do, you will suffer opportunity loss to your margins in the meantime and long-lasting damage to your reputation for reliability and consistency.

Damage control is always more expensive than value control. One way or the other, you will pay for value. It is always less expensive to safeguard your values than to try to turn them around after they have become jeopardized.

Controlling your values means managing your business as if your customers were in charge of your TVC (total value control). This simply acknowledges reality. Your customers control your values—how much they are, how soon they take effect, and how sure they must be—by the premium margins they are predisposed to pay for their advantages. You are unlikely, and certainly unwise, to invest in more value or different values than your customers can implement, or values whose impact in customer perceptions is unduly delayed or unreliable. The values you must sponsor are the values you can sell at maximum margins, and these are already the values your customers control.

By giving your customers the controlling interest in managing your values, you can avoid the twin pitfalls of undervaluing and overvaluing your contributions to their competitive advantage. Of the two, overvaluing is the likelier and also the costlier. If you are a manufacturer or processor, and especially if you produce high technology equipment, systems, and networks, you are a perpetual candidate for engineering your values over and above your customers' "good enough" standards. Each time you succumb to the temptation to believe that "the value is in the box" and you make it faster, smaller, or more powerful just because you can, you will be a value-overadder.

Your customers will be unable to use your excess value. They will be unwilling to retrain their people to implement it and to connect it to their existing systems where it may interrupt or obsolete long-established processes. As a result, they will not repay you for your overcosted investment with the superpremium margins that would be required.

Value that you allow to walk away from your control

after you have paid for it is unaffordable. Value that you allow to elude your customers' control because they are unable to make advantageous use of it after they have paid for it is unforgivable.

Helping Customers Stay in Control

A business is "in control" when its managers are controlling their values well enough to guarantee their muchness and soonness. They are, in brief, *sure* of their values. Conversely, a business is "out of control" when its managers can no longer be sure of their values or when they do not know their values and therefore cannot price them or sell them. As soon as value control slips or slides, margin control goes with it.

Why would a manager voluntarily relinquish control of his business, which is the inevitable result of losing control of the sureness of his or her values that permit margin control, to customers or competitors? The more driven he or she is by a product or process, the easier it will be to believe that performance values must be the basis of price rather than the financial values that enable products and processes to contribute to a customer's competitive advantage.

This kind of mindset "comes with the territory" in many industries: high technology electronics hardware and software businesses that sell "boxes," "programs," and "systems"; telecommunications businesses that sell "switches" and "usage"; biochemical businesses that sell "antibodies" and biomedical businesses that sell "pumps and syringes"; petrochemical businesses that sell "pounds," "gallons," and "tank cars"; capital equipment businesses that sell "earthmovers and backhoes" or "generators" or "pollution control systems."

In the same mindset are steel companies that sell "tons"; brewers who sell "barrels"; millers who work with "one hand on the mill and the other held up to God"; and insurance companies that sell "policies."

These are the businesses whose managers worry more

about their own competitors than the competitors of their customers. When a customer of one of these businesses gets into trouble, he comes to his suppliers with the only solution they have taught him: "If you are having cash flow problems or your margins are being driven down," customers have been taught, "come to us and drive our margins down too. Then all of us—you, we, and the suppliers who serve us, whom we will go to in the same way—can share negative growth."

When you are in control of your values, you can dedicate your business to keeping your customers valuable; that is, able to use your values to make themselves advantaged instead of depleting your margins to make themselves survivable. You cannot manage their businesses for them. But you must help them manage the critical success factors in their critical functions or critical lines of business that are your markets. This is the responsibility of every marketer. Their prosperity is every bit as vital to you as it is to them. Both of you sink or swim with their prosperity.

Just as your customers control your values by what they are satisfied with and what they are not, you must help control the sureness of their competitive advantage in the critical operations of their businesses that provide your mutual life-blood. This is the overarching objective of your business that your mission statement should be committed to. It is also the platform for your business partnerships: two businesses committed to the competitive advantage of each other through the exchange of critical values.

Practicing the Control You Preach

As customer industries mature, you will see new practices and procedures, policies, and products introduced with increasing frequency to reduce margin pressure and keep costs under control. You must make sure that you are a part of these solutions. What are you doing to help customers retain or regain their margins? How are you helping them to keep a tight rein on costs? If the only ways you have to do these

things are to lower your own cost through dealing and
discounting, you will end up in the same fix. Neither of you
will be adding value to the other.

The flip side of the situation is that you will be called on
by maturing customers to provide increased free services in
order to protect your partnerships with them. This will
entice you to adopt excessive costs and inefficiencies in your
own business. To insure yourself against excess, you should
develop standard values for your major services so that you
can check them off against questions like these:

- What is necessary and what is nice?
- What is the acceptable standard of value for each
  necessary service and are we practicing within it?
- Do red flags automatically go up when we deviate
  from our standards on the side of excess?

If you screen them for customer value, you are likely to
find that many of the services you are providing as alleged
additions to customer competitiveness are unnecessary.
Their contributions may be insignificant to your customers
and cost-ineffective for you. If you have a system for detect-
ing variances from your standards, you will be alerted to the
outflow of dollars that do not contribute at least a dollar's
worth of value to your customers. Fewer than 20 percent of
all your investments will account for up to 80 percent of your
low-value or no-value services. Most managers will not know
that they are spending excessively compared to the contributions they are making to customer value. Other managers
will know that there are better places to invest your money
but they will be playing it safe on the theory that "if it doesn't
hurt, it might do some good."

Value control must be based on explicit guidelines for
value creation and delivery by your managers. The guidelines should inform them on necessity and appropriateness:
the necessary minimum values to ensure your cost-effectiveness and the appropriate ranges of values within which your
competitive advantage can be maintained.

Products and services that are of insufficient value

should become an endangered species. You should take the same point of view toward your managers. On the one hand, 20 percent or fewer of them will account for up to 80 percent of the values your customers derive from you. On the other hand are the 20 percent who cause up to 80 percent of all the variations from your standards of value. When you can measure their contributions, you can teach them that there are better ways to do things or better things to do. Unless you take remedial action, the 20 percent who are deviates will eventually nullify the 20 percent who support your business by creating its values. You will be your own worst competitor.

Projecting Your Value Into New-Wave Selling

Controlling your value is controlling your business destiny. As the supplier-customer relationship evolves into new-wave forms of buying and selling, your control strategies are destined to change with them. Your value as a *supplier* will be progressively supplanted by your value as an *applier* and, after that, by your value as a manager of *multisupplier* products and applications. Your ability to add value by managing critical customer functions and lines of business will be the acid test of your knowledge of customer businesses and your skills at improving their competitive advantage.

If you know enough about customer functions or business lines to be able to affect their contributions to costs and revenues, you may also know how to manage function or business lines cost-effectively. To do so, you need to have three types of knowledge:

1. Customer business knowledge, both operational and financial
2. Project or facility management knowledge
3. Multivendor knowledge of competitors and allied suppliers

By combining these skill sets, you can extend your value by offering customers a "buy" instead of "make" alternative

to managing one of their cost or profit centers. If you take
on this role, you free yourself from having to sell your values
over and over again with each sale. Instead, you will be able
to resell them annually as a contract manager rather than as
an optional source of supply. Under contract, your products
and services, along with compatible multivendor products
and services, will jointly contribute to your overall *value under
management*. You will not have to price them or propose them.
You will simply have to make sure that each of them is the
best value contributor for its job.

As a de facto customer-function or business-line manager, you will be held responsible for controlling the value
of your contributions to total customer profits. Your cost-
benefit analysis will be the crux of your management contract, in which you propose the muchness and soonness of
your contribution. On a comparative basis, your contribution
will have to exceed the value that a customer can manage to
produce himself or that other contract managers can reliably
propose.

In consumer packaged goods businesses, contract management is known as *category management* of a retailer's costs
and revenues in a major category of his business. Philip
Morris and Johnson & Johnson act as managers for their
product categories sold through major supermarket mer-
chandisers, Philip Morris in cigarettes and J&J in health and
beauty aids. Each of them contracts with chain stores to
manage their own category, controlling stocking and shelving, inventory flow, and promotions. They also manage sales
through advertising and promotions like coupon merchan-
dising, as well as making sure that the optimal mix of multivendor products, including their own, is maintained at all
times.

In industrial and technology-based businesses as well as
services, contract management is known as *facility management*
of a customer's business operation. IBM and Digital Equipment Corporation act as facility managers for computer-
based information systems. Each of them contracts with
customers to integrate their systems with multivendor products and services; control their staffing, equipment, service,

and maintenance; and provide progressive upgrading of the facility they manage as the state of their art matures.

When an industry you supply converts to category or facility management, you will face a conflict of values:

- Should you become a manager or be managed by a competitor?
- Should you become an integrator or be one of several suppliers whose products and services are integrated by a competitor who is?

Because facility managers and system integrators are closer to their customers in the value chain than product and service suppliers, their value is greater and their partnerships are more closely held. A facility manager controls the values he manages. As long as a customer's return on his investment is satisfactory, Philip Morris products can receive more preferential shelf space in its managed categories than the competing products of R. J. Reynolds, American Tobacco Company, Lorillard, and Brown & Williamson, and IBM equipment and services can dominate the systems it integrates in its managed facilities.

As either a category or facility manager, you circumvent comparative product merits and their price considerations as constraints on selling. You partner with your customers by playing a parallel role in their business management, acting in their place. They will assess you on your contribution the same way they assess their own managers: Are you maximizing the value you contribute at the minimal cost and can they absolutely, positively rely on banking your proposed contributions?

Seizing the Value Initiative

In the give-and-take value exchange of supplier-customer business partnerships, "what if-ing" of more and faster-acting values goes on all the time. Customers are factor-smart. They know the critical success factors that benefit or detract from their functions and lines of business. You must be equally factor-smart about your customers' businesses. If you expect customers to know their own business, you will not be disappointed. They must not be disappointed, either, when they expect you to add value to them because you know the businesses of many customers and can therefore see each one of them through the magnified perspective of all of them.

This is the competitive advantage granted to value-based suppliers: to see each individual customer in the context of the customer industry's values and to be able to help each customer improve his competitiveness within that context.

Because of this grand perspective, customers have a right to expect you to take the initiative in the mutual value-improvement process. They expect, in other words, that you will make adding values to them your business and that you are expert in it.

Making and marketing whatever it is they make and market is your customers' business. Adding values to what they make and how they make it and market it is your business. This is what it means to be a value-based supplier.

If you could get inside the heads of your customers' managers, this is how they might challenge you to seize the value initiative with them:

> You are the expert in adding value to critical success factors in my industry like the factor I manage in my function or line of business. In general, I think we do a pretty good job. But I am being called on by my managers to do an even better job, and quickly. Some of our competitors are pulling ahead of us. We have to catch up. Our customers are getting fussier about what they need to satisfy them, probably because their own managers are coming down on them the same way my managers are coming down on me.
>
> So far, you've shown me your norms for my operations. You've held their templates over my costs and revenues and productivity and you've told me that I'm out of line here, over or under there, and you've given me a rough idea about how much I'm over or under in

each case. On the assumption that you know what you're doing, that your norms have the basis in fact that you say they do, you apparently see areas for improvement that I could deal with cost-effectively and that would show up in a reasonable amount of time in my contribution. In rank order of importance, what are they?

At this point, you are on the verge of one or more leads. You are being invited to sell your value. Where do you begin? You can say:

What if we were to start with this cost—or rather, this network of costs, because they are interconnected? What if we were to start with this sales region or this customer industry? Here is where you stand now. Here is where our norms say you can be. Let us calculate the added value to you of each one percent improvement we can make by helping you grow from where you are now to where you can be. For each percentage point of improvement, we will ask you what it will be worth to you. When you arrive at a significant amount of value, and what it is worth to you appears to be in a cost-effective ratio to it, ask us *how* we can proceed together.

When the customer asks, "How?" you have uncovered a qualified and quantified lead. At this point, you can begin the second phase of the what-if process:

What if we add this, substitute this for that, eliminate this, leave that unchanged? What performance improvements will that add? What are their financial contributions? How much cost does it reduce or how much new revenues and earnings does it add? How long does it take? What if we make this incremental change? Now what are the operating and financial advantages to your competitiveness?

As a value-adder, you will become known by the quality of your what-ifs. But their quantity is important too. You should have a what-if with you at all times, based on your norms and your knowledge of your customer businesses. In the words of American Express: Don't leave home without it.

Index